WAR AND WHEAT

NAVIGATING MARKETS
DURING GLOBAL
CONFLICT

DENNIS VOZNESENSKI

Published by the Power Writers Publishing Group in 2024.

Dennis Voznesenski copyright 2024.

All Rights Reserved. No part of this book may be reproduced by any mechanical, photographic, or electronic processes, or in the form of a phonographic recording. Nor may it be stored in a retrieval system, transmitted or otherwise copied for public or private use other than for 'fair use' as brief quotations embodied in articles and reviews, without prior written permission of the publisher.

 A catalogue record for this work is available from the National Library of Australia

ISBN: 978-1-7635809-3-0 (pbk)
ISBN: 978-1-7635809-4-7 (ebk)

Cover design by Publicious Book Publishing
Internal layout by Publicious Book Publishing
www.publicious.com.au

Disclaimer
Any opinions expressed in this work are exclusively those of the author and are not necessarily the views held or endorsed by others quoted throughout. All of the information, exercises and concepts contained within the publication are intended for general information only. The author does not take any responsibility for any choices that any individual or organization may make relating to this information in the business, personal, financial, familial, or other areas of life. If any individual or organization does wish to implement the ideas discussed herein, it is recommended that they obtain their own independent advice specific to their circumstances.

CONTENTS

Introduction: Why did I write this book?...................... i

Chapter 1: World War I – War Goes Global 1

Chapter 2: World War II – The Curse of Australia
is Procrastination 43

Chapter 3: From COVID to Ukraine – A New
Global Conflict is Brewing 104

Conclusion: 'History Doesn't Repeat Itself,
But it Often Rhymes'.. 127

Questions and Answers with Dennis 133

Acknowledgements 135

Notes 137

About the Author

During his career Dennis Voznesenski has engaged with the world's largest grain merchants, food manufacturers, biofuel producers and farmers. While working for the largest agricultural bank in the world, Dennis covered the Australian grains sector from Sydney before heading over to London to cover the global grains market.

Dennis has appeared across CNBC, BBC World News, Al Jazeera and most Australian TV channels. He has had work referenced across The Financial Times, New York Times, the Economist, the Australian, Australian Financial Review, Bloomberg, and Reuters.

INTRODUCTION

INTRODUCTION

Why did I write this book?

Why I wrote this book is a great question. The answer is simple. Curiosity. When I started working in the grains industry as a junior commodity analyst, I was fascinated by why markets moved in the way they did. I trawled through years of historic data, trying to decipher why global commodity prices jumped on particular days and on others they barely budged. I found that the largest and most sudden price changes in history were caused most frequently by politics and wars.

During a war, there's not much a market can hide. The reasons behind price moves are laid bare and appear surprisingly straight forward. Wars also offer up other secrets. They provide a unique window into the vulnerabilities of an industry, and consequently the country that it operates in.

Not only does this book offer a unique perspective on how wars interfere with markets, but it does so through the unique lens of Australia. While World War I and World War II were before my time, I turned to the records that remained. I read more than 3,000 newspaper articles from those two periods, and was able to assess the shifts in markets day by day.

WAR AND WHEAT

The last section of this book deals with all the major events that led up to the war in Ukraine and the war itself. These are events that took place while I was already working in the industry. From the once in a century Australian drought between 2017 and 2019, to the once in a century pandemic between 2019 and 2021, to the once in a century disruption to global grain markets due to the war in Ukraine. I had my finger on the pulse working through it all.

I was incredibly fortunate to see these events from a number of unique angles. During the once in a century drought, I worked for a company that oversaw a very broad spectrum of the Australian supply chain, from the nation's largest farmers to its grain merchants. The stress the drought forced upon the market allowed me to understand how the industry functioned at its limits. I was able to see what happened when wheat started to run out in the country.

During the pandemic and the war in Ukraine, I worked for the largest agricultural bank in the world, both in Australia and in London. I was able to see how COVID-19 ground the world to a complete halt, and what the impact was. Not only that, but I was able to engage with the world's largest food companies in the process. When the war in Ukraine broke out, my job and network allowed me to assess both the Australian and global impact.

I didn't intend to write this book initially; oddly enough it in a way wrote itself. The stories and lessons that unintentionally came out of my research of markets in WWI and WWII were simply too interesting not to share with you. Whether you are a farmer, a grain trader, a food manufacturer, a fund manager, a biofuel

INTRODUCTION

producer, a politician, or you simply eat bread - this book will offer you an unparalleled understanding of markets during conflict.

For the Australian grains industry, the key takeaway of this book is simple. The vulnerabilities the industry had leading into both world wars are the exact same ones that exist now. The industry is woefully unprepared for future conflict.

CHAPTER ONE

World War I – War Goes Global

WWI started in late July of 1914. Austria-Hungary had just declared war on Serbia following the assassination of Archduke Franz Ferdinand. The German Empire declared war on Tsarist Russia, Belgium and France, and soon-after, the United Kingdom declared war on Germany.

The initial military flashpoint hovered over Serbia, Austria, Bulgaria, Romania, and Russia. Together, just these initial warring countries constituted nearly a quarter of the world's 111 million tonnes of wheat production. Despite entering the war with abundant global wheat reserves, a combination of fear, government stockpiling and supply chain disruptions put a rocket under global markets.

News of war led to wild trading in US wheat markets, a bellwether for global prices. Prices whipsawed violently from day-to-day on news of potential truce, followed by news of talks breaking down. Many US grain merchants who shorted markets on the initial war news, assuming a fast resolve to the war, suffered heavy losses and even bankruptcies as prices moved higher.

Wheat prices rose even faster in the UK, due to both its proximity to the war and high dependence on imports. London alone had to feed over 7 million

WAR AND WHEAT

people, and relied on 1 million tonnes of wheat imports arriving by sea every year. Consumer food hoarding was prevalent.[1] The government attempted to calm panic buying in the initial months of the war by stating that multiple months of wheat reserves would be available following the domestic harvest, but large ques persisted.[2] The UK's food challenges were exacerbated by one of the worst droughts on record crippling Australia's upcoming wheat crop. Prior to the war, Australia supplied just over a tenth of the UK's wheat imports.[3]

News travels slow

13,000 km south of continental Europe, signs of what was soon to come was slow to make its way into Australian newspapers. Only hints trickled down from week to week in the lead up to the war beginning. One month prior to the breakout of WWI, the Australian government raised taxes, and commentators were sarcastically suggesting that the government was raising taxes as though they were preparing for a war or famine. It turned out that both were true.

When the official declaration of war came, farmers in Australia were three months away from starting to harvest one of the smallest wheat crops in over a decade due to drought. It turned out to be a mere 680,000 tonnes, an astounding 75% down on the previous year.[4] To make matters worse, news of stronger prices in Europe and the United States led farmers and grain merchants in Australia to withhold wheat from sale in the hope of benefiting from higher prices later. This knock-on effect, on top of already limited supplies for local flour millers and bakers, led to concern in parliament.

WORLD WAR I – WAR GOES GLOBAL

In early September 1914, as wheat reserves started running low, a dozen large merchants were publicly named and shamed in national newspapers for speculating at the expense of the country. The merchants were said to be controlling the majority of remaining wheat stocks, and holding it back from sale. Australian wheat prices escalated by a mind-boggling 62% between July and September.[5]

As it had in the US, the strong price rise caught a number of grain merchants off guard. Some of the speculative Australian grain merchants were betting through US wheat futures markets that the war would be finished quickly, and prices would fall. If only they were right! It wasn't long before creditors were being called in to deal with a series of bankruptcies as prices continued to rise.

Higher wheat prices were threatening to soon translate into rising flour costs for bakers. Prior to September 1914, bakers were using cheaper flour stocks bought earlier in the year and refrained from buying new supplies at war level pricing. Their hope was that the war would quickly end, and prices would decline. At the same time, flour millers were using cheaper wheat stocks that were bought prior to the war, but were also quickly running out. The government feared that soon flour millers would raise the price of flour and bakers would need to raise the price of bread for consumers.

The situation quickly became desperate. Flour millers were not only competing against one another for the remaining wheat supplies in Australia, but they also had to compete with an unprecedented export market sucking wheat out of Australia. Remaining local supplies rapidly flowed out of Australia as foreign buyers, particularly governments from war-torn Europe,

WAR AND WHEAT

paid substantial premiums over what the local Australian private sector could afford.

Pressure was building on the Australian government to create a solution to the quickly disappearing wheat stocks. So, on the 10th of September the federal government issued a proclamation prohibiting all exports of wheat and flour, except to the United Kingdom. The ban was marketed as being a precautionary measure to avoid inadvertently selling food to the enemy through neutral countries like Denmark or the Netherlands. This followed revelations that for several months prior to the outbreak of hostilities, two-thirds of the wheat exported from Canada's port of Montreal went to Rotterdam and Antwerp before being transferred to Germany. While concrete data on the volume of wheat that found its way to the new enemy was not available, Canadian officials came to the conclusion that Germany was probably preparing for a war of at least one year's duration.[6]

Despite the export ban, local prices remained high. A combination of the drought and the large quantities of wheat that had already left Australia's shores prior to the ban meant that there was barely anything left. The government's attention turned to limiting bread price rises in any way it could. Food riots were the last thing needed when the nation was already on edge. A royal commission was set up to inquire with the grains industry if it would be reasonable to implement a maximum wheat price of 4s 2d per bushel ('s' stands for shillings, 'd' stands for pence), a level that the free market had already surpassed by 20%.

Initially, New South Wales (NSW), the nation's largest wheat producing state at the time, was hesitant to implement unilateral price controls on its own without nation-wide coordination. The NSW government

WORLD WAR I – WAR GOES GLOBAL

rightfully feared that if it implemented a maximum wheat price on its own, wheat would flow over the border to other states where a higher free market price prevailed. However, concerns over the public reaction to rising food prices outweighed these fears, and despite industry pushback, the NSW government moved to implement a maximum price on all already harvested wheat.

By the end of September 1914, wheat stocks in NSW were reportedly just under 100,000 tonnes. At the time, the state required 25,000 tonnes a month to feed the population, meaning there was a mere four months of stock available before the pantry would be completely bare.[7] Given that the harvest was only 1-2 months away, in theory, there should have been enough wheat. However, while officially there was 100,000 tonnes left, far less of that was readily accessible. Some of the stock might have been sitting in farm sheds in the middle of rural Australia, or in a distant storage facility, or simply not fit for human consumption.

Following the implementation of a maximum price for what wheat could be sold for, the buying and selling of grain came to a grinding halt. Buyers of wheat were plenty but could only offer the set government maximum price which sellers were unwilling to sell for. Millers who were desperately short of wheat were rumoured to be buying it at above government-imposed rates on a newly developing black-market, but the activity was limited over fears that the government would confiscate the transacted product. Certain bakers in country districts started charging higher prices for bread than that fixed by the government, but were duly informed that they would be prosecuted if they did not lower their prices.

Flour millers made it clear to the government that with their stocks of cheaper wheat running very low, they would soon be forced to move on to more expensive stock. That would leave them with no choice but to raise the price of flour that bakers would have to pay them. Meanwhile, bakers claimed that either flour prices had to decline, or they wouldn't be able to bake without increasing bread prices for consumers.

On this news, in a show of force the government moved on Darling Island grain stores (located in present day Darling Harbour in Sydney), and confiscated 140,000 bags of wheat from the storage facility of a grain merchant. Rumours were that the merchant was planning to export the wheat in the coming days.[8]

Many merchants continued to simply refuse to sell their wheat. They hoped that by refusing to sell, the grains industry could bend the government into rolling back its maximum price measure. The government then began to frequently authorise the seizure and distribution of wheat as required. From that point onwards, flourmill operators applied to the government for wheat to meet their immediate requirements. The government then confiscated or issued a 'forced sale' requirement on grain merchants. At the time, the only wheat that was meant to be confiscated was the stock that was owned by grain merchants. However, it soon turned out that part of the already confiscated wheat was actually grain being stored by grain merchants on behalf of farmers.

The industry demands answers from the government

Grain merchants, flour millers and farmers demanded that the government be clear on the next maximum price it would set for the new season's wheat that was about to be harvested from October. By this point the wheat trade in effect had stalled. No one was willing to create new contracts for the wheat about to be harvested in fear of new government regulations cancelling contracts.

By early October, some of the other states also implemented maximum wheat prices. Some states introduced higher prices than NSW and claimed they were accommodating for the fact that they were more drought-hit and hence needed more support. The result was that speculators or merchants would be able to sell wheat sourced in NSW for higher prices in other states. As a result, NSW began plans to ban interstate wheat movements and trade. The plan to ban started a long battle between the states, with claims of the interstate trade bans being unconstitutional.

The Australian government starts preparing to supply the war effort

With war showing no signs of concluding, it dawned on both the Australian and British governments that the global wheat crop would be reduced substantially due to the war. At the same time, import volumes into Europe would rocket higher to feed allied troops.

The Australian government quickly started planning to open up vast tracts of land for agriculture ahead of next year's planting in April. This included almost six hundred thousand hectares in northern NSW. To put the magnitude in context, the total wheat area in NSW in the previous season was only just over 1 million hectares.[4] In Canada, the government moved in the same direction, opening almost 200,000 additional hectares of land for the cultivation of wheat to supply the UK's needs. Meanwhile, India planned to increase the area dedicated to wheat planting by 13%.[9]

To encourage as much planting as possible across Australia, the government also began pressuring banks to ease lending requirements to farmers. The government asked the banks to advance money to farmers for crop planting, with the government guaranteeing 20% of the loan amount for farmers with insufficient financial security. Farmers who had enough security were asked to go to the banks on their own.

In order to incentivise farmers to take up the new opened lands and cultivate them early in the new year, the government started formulating a guaranteed minimum price to be paid to farmers for their wheat. The minimum price would need to cover all their costs and allow farmers to make a reasonable return. The farmer groups advised the government that subsidising tillage costs in order to increase the area wheat could be grown on was the best support for them. But they also added that there was little they could do if the drought continued.

Hesitancy among farmers to expand the area they were cultivating was also rife due to outstanding bank debts. Many farmers were already in their second or third consecutive year of drought. Planting another large crop would expose them to an even bigger debt burden and risk their farms being foreclosed on if another poor harvest eventuated.

Government plans to increase production didn't stop at simply opening new lands for farmers to cultivate, and providing financial support. Aware of the slow uptake to cultivate new land, the government started making plans to take the unprecedented next step of clearing land and growing wheat itself. Their plan included hiring labour for the project which they claimed would simultaneously reduce unemployment. As a starting point, the government selected 20,000 hectares of land in central NSW to cultivate.

Rain finally arrives

In the middle of October, local newspapers were reporting that the drought had finally broken following significant rainfall over much of the east coast of Australia. The rain supported wheat crops still in the ground and prospects for planting in early 1915. Soil moisture had improved substantially.

The government was aware that local supply would very likely improve next season and proposed paying only 4s per bushel for wheat grown on new land. That was notably lower than the most recent price of 5s per bushel in the free market. The government's argument was that the price was still above the pre-war and pre-drought market levels.

Warring in Europe ramps up

On the 31st of October 1914, the Ottoman empire (present day Türkiye) joined the war on the side of the Central Powers, led by Germany, and blockaded the Dardanelles. The Dardanelles were the only route available for Russian wheat to make its way from the Black Sea to allied countries - specifically the UK and France. In early November 1914, two Turkish destroyers shelled the present-day port of Odessa in

Ukraine, and Chicago wholesale wheat prices jumped 5% in a single day.[10] At that point, Russia accounted for just over a fifth of all global wheat exports. Adding to the sudden bullishness in global prices, reports started coming in of drought impacting crops in Canada and Argentina, leaving only India and the US with any sizeable wheat production prospects and stock levels.

The Australian government gets heavy handed

Back in Australia, the government got even more heavy handed in the leadup to the Christmas of 1914. While it was understood that the coming small harvest would be sufficient to supply the needs of NSW, it was feared that Australia as a whole would be in a shortage for the coming year. On the 27th of November, the federal government proposed a bill to create a board of five individuals who could declare any wheat to be the property of the crown at a new higher fixed rate of 5s per bushel.[11] The intention of the higher price was to cancel out the social negativity associated with forcefully taking farmer' wheat. Taking wheat directly from farmers like this was the most heavy-handed approach proposed to solve the shortage to date.

The federal government started hastily pushing through the bill in late November 1914. All pre-war contracts entered into by growers were to be cancelled under the proposed legislation. If they were not cancelled, the government was concerned that wheat farmers would be forced to sell their wheat to grain merchants and millers on contracted lower pre-war prices while having to buy war-level priced seed wheat, fuel and fertiliser for planting in early 1915. The government feared that the low prices in the pre-war contracts would stymie the farmers' ability to expand their wheat planting and hence supply the wheat desperately needed by the British government.

Under the proposed bill, the cost of a loaf of bread would be increased to accommodate the higher price millers had to pay for wheat, and bakers had to pay for flour. The bottom line was that despite the government's best efforts, consumer prices would have to rise to ensure flour millers and bakers could continue to operate.

The passing of the bill started to look certain by the middle of December 1914. Despite the NSW government warning that wheat found in transit moving towards the Victorian border would be confiscated, farmers in NSW continued to truck their wheat south. Farmers were not interested in waiting to hear whether the bill would pass and if they would lose ownership of their wheat. Farmers were selling thousands of bags of wheat to Victorian buyers where there was no maximum price mandated yet. There was not a single spare truck available on the NSW/Victorian border. By the 11th of December the bill to take ownership of all wheat was passed in parliament. The governor's signature was the last requirement for the bill to pass into law.

The situation got so tense at one point between states that the Commonwealth Government charged NSW with infringing on the constitution by banning wheat exports to other states. The claim was overruled by the high court which stated that the Commonwealth Government was overstepping its powers.

Grain merchants meet to discuss the cancelling of contracts on 'gentlemen's terms'

The challenge faced by NSW grain merchants was that all of their contracts with farmers would soon be voided by the government. That meant they couldn't execute contracted and planned wheat deliveries within their own state or into other states to flour millers or other grain merchants. Those who were in NSW and already physically had the wheat that they pre-sold to Victorian merchants, were banned from moving it across the border. At a meeting of the largest NSW and Victorian grain merchants, it was found that 250,000 pounds (or AUD 35 million in 2023 currency), was owed by NSW grain merchants to their Victorian counterparts.

For the grain merchants who bet incorrectly against the market on the assumption that the war would be over quickly, the government's annulment of contracts was a godsend. On the other hand, for the millers who purchased wheat from traders at cheaper pre-war levels, the ruling meant that they would have to re-enter the market and buy at a higher price. Some contract counterparties were able to come to a gentlemen's agreement and 'washout' the contracts that were in place, while others were left disgruntled.

On December 25th a bill was signed into law that made all wheat become the property of the crown. Under the new law, farmers' wheat was to be taken as required with a set price being paid in exchange for it.

WORLD WAR I – WAR GOES GLOBAL

Shortly after, parliament was informed of the remaining shortfall that would need to be imported, and the price was expected to be 6s 6d per bushel (remember, locally they were paying farmers 5s at the time). The last time wheat was imported into Australia was in 1903 during the federation drought. Wheat was imported from San Francisco in the US, and Buenos Ayres in Argentina at an average price of 4s 3d. This average price was used as an argument by the government to justify why the 5s minimum price they were offering farmers to seize their wheat was generous. However, it turned out that the price during the federation drought rose even as high as 6s 5d, a fact conveniently left out when the maximum price setting committee argued for the 5s price in parliament.

While importing wheat may seem straightforward, it is anything but that during a war. The world was suddenly and critically short of available shipping capacity. Ships were either being requisitioned by governments for military use, sunk by German submarines, or vessel operators were simply hesitant to bring vessels to Australia in fear of them being requisitioned by the Australian government. Both shipping rates and shipping insurance skyrocketed, adding a substantial cost to importing wheat that the Australian government and the taxpayer would have to foot the bill for.

When the government was criticised by grain merchants and farmers for banning the export of wheat and subduing price upside for farmers as a result, the government argued that if it hadn't put the ban in place, it would have needed to import even more wheat. Furthermore, taxpayers would have needed to foot an even bigger bill for imported wheat when all available resources were needed for the war effort. Wheat imports in 1903 unfolded at great cost to taxpayers. At the time, exporters were moving wheat reserves out of the country for a high price while local stocks dwindled.

1915 – Panic, shortages and unprecedented action

1915 started much like 1914 had ended. There was grave concern around local Australian wheat supplies, and global prices were skyrocketing. By February 1915, Chicago wheat prices were up almost 100% compared to the price at the start of the war.[10] London wheat prices were reaching record highs, India moved to ban all wheat exports except to the United Kingdom until the end of the year, and food riots broke out in Spain.

Flour millers in Germany and Austria were starting to mix bread flour with the likes of rye and corn due to a British blockade of continental Europe. Meanwhile, Russia had a large surplus of grain and was contracted to supply the French with 400,000 tonnes of wheat, but with the closing of the Dardanelles, there was no way of moving product out of the Black Sea. The only option for Russia was to export through its northern ports which was incredibly slow and inefficient, and during winter it was impossible because of the harsh conditions. Most of Russia's wheat was grown further south.

In Australia, the situation with scarce local supplies was becoming worse. When the NSW government announced plans to ship wheat to New Zealand, which was also short of supplies, the federal Attorney General temporarily seized the stock at the port of

WORLD WAR I – WAR GOES GLOBAL

Sydney, before having the decision overturned. The federal government was busy setting the groundwork for wheat to be imported into Australia from the US and Argentina. To the governments surprise, it turned out that there were two fully loaded German vessels at anchor in Sumatra that were initially headed for Europe from Sydney and Melbourne before the war began. No one knew why they stopped there, but the shortage of supplies in Australia resulted in the wheat being shipped back to Australia and purchased by a Victorian buyer.

Notwithstanding the rare occasions when Australian wheat was sent to regions in desperate need, like the starving Belgians under German occupation, wheat continued to be held in Australia strictly for local use.

A hungry UK heads to Gallipoli to free the Dardanelles

A shortage of food played a notable role when the legendary Gallipoli campaign was being thought through by the British government and its allies in March 1915. UK food prices were running rampant, increasing by 13% in just the previous three months. At that time, Argentina was a large source of wheat for the British. However, their stocks were starting to run low due to strong exports and poor production. Meanwhile, Australia's last crop was drought stricken. The possibility of higher food prices and the impending need to implement tighter controls over food consumption at home helped the British decide to send its own and Australian troops, with support from France, to free up the Dardanelles. Freeing up the Dardanelles would allow large volumes of piled up Russian wheat to flow through to allies. The campaign concluded without achieving its objectives in January 1916.

Logistical challenges curtail benefit of a large Australian crop

In April 1915, with seasonal conditions continuing to improve across Australia, the government's initiatives to increase the amount of planted area to wheat was on track. Data suggests that the wheat area sown rose by an astronomical 30%.[4] While the rise in wheat planting was exactly what the government was aiming for, the soon-to-be felt logistical challenges around handling a record harvest later in the year soon began to dawn on the government.

The challenges would range from insufficient truck and rail capacity to carry so much wheat from rural areas to ocean ports, to a shortage of freight globally to ship wheat from the ports. There were even unexpected issues like a lack of bags to transport the wheat in. The UK government had put a 'first call' on all of the grain sacks that were being produced in India, leaving Australia out in the cold to find its own. Most wheat production was typically moved significant distances in bags by truck to rail sites or port. To limit the expected logistical challenges of moving grain to ports, the government hired thousands of workers to extend rail lines into newly open lands, to be ready when harvest started in October.

The federal government then organised a set of 'super-middlemen' to firstly organise moving harvested grain from rural areas to ports, and then to export it out of Australia. Dreyfus and Co and Darling and

WORLD WAR I – WAR GOES GLOBAL

Sons were given the rights to coordinate the business of buying grain from farmers. While Elders Smith and Co, and a company called Gibbs, Bright and Co, received exclusive rights to charter vessels for the shipping of the harvest overseas. The aim of centralising the organisation of shipping was to avoid state governments bidding against one another for freight from overseas vessel owners. A bidding war between the states would raise the price of freight and reduce the price the Australian government would receive for its wheat while apportioning more profit to ship owners.

The government ruled on the fees the companies in the supply chain could earn for moving grain from the farms to the ports. The core aim was to ensure that everyone along the supply chain, from farmers to grain merchants, stayed employed and active, and that the industry didn't fall into disarray.

In case you're wondering what would have happened if the government didn't intervene in the markets at all, the lack of sufficient logistical capacity to move and export a crop of this size would have brought the industry to its knees. A large harvest would quickly overwhelm the logistical capacity that was geared to moving grain to ports by truck and rail from rural areas. The lack of spare freight space would result in farmers bidding prices lower against one another to sell their harvest to merchants with remaining ability to move wheat to port. Eventually, with freight capacity full for the foreseeable future, demand from grain merchants would dry up entirely.

Further down the supply chain, smaller merchants based at ports, without the ability to charter a vessel, would try to sell their grain to the few larger merchants who had managed to charter ships for export. In effect leading to the same situation that the farmers had to deal with that I described in the paragraph above. Smaller merchants would bid against each other to sell the grain to larger merchants who had freight space on the ship. In the process, prices would decline until margins were squeezed to the extent that it no longer made sense to sell their grain.

Meanwhile, the grain merchants who were large enough to charter a vessel from overseas vessel owners would bid against one another for the remaining available vessels until their own margins were squeezed to virtually nothing.

The only ones in the supply chain who could make money (and exorbitant amounts of it) were those who owned vessels that they could rent out. The bottom line was that the absence of government intervention would have resulted in the industry as a whole suffering severely. If prices collapsed, farm bankruptcies would have skyrocketed. The following season, production would fall substantially, and many farmers may have left the industry all together. Considering how important food production was as part of the economy, as part of national security and in supporting the allied effort, this scenario could not be allowed to happen.

By late September 1915, the Australian harvest was still at least a month away from starting. The coming harvest was at this point estimated to be 2.7 million tonnes. After removing 1 million tonnes for domestic consumption, it was estimated that it would still take 400-600 ships to carry the surplus overseas.

By October 1915, overseas ship owners were becoming reluctant to allow their vessels to go to

WORLD WAR I – WAR GOES GLOBAL

Australia to pick up or drop off goods. The vessel owners increasingly feared that their ships would be requisitioned by the government.

Meanwhile, the Baltic exchange in Greece, a large freight exchange, vocalised its dissatisfaction with the Australian proposal that involved two designated companies being responsible for organising all of the grain shipments from the country. Their dissatisfaction stemmed from the fact that instead of dealing with individual smaller companies in Australia, overseas ship owners would now have to deal with a government backed organisation with far greater bargaining power.

In November, the Commonwealth government announced that 300,000 tonnes of freight had been secured for shipment between December 1915 and February 1916 via two of the largest global shippers at the time.[13] While this seemed like a significant amount at first, in reality it was insufficient given the exportable surplus of around 1.7 million tonnes that was being expected from the crop that was about to be harvested. Interestingly, the freight cost agreed to by the government was 11% below spot market rates, and not significantly in excess of freight prices that were seen during other large production years where freight was in high demand.

While the achievement of locking in cheaper rates seemed like a good outcome at first, it soon created headaches for the government. Despite their contractual obligations, in the coming months foreign ship owners began refusing to move forward with the agreement, especially as freight availability became scarcer. Towards the end of 1915, 3,000 freight vessels accounting for 4,000,000 tonnes of capacity, mostly British and German, were reportedly sunk. To make it easier for countries supplying food to the UK, the British government had to pass a law prohibiting British ships from carrying cargo solely between foreign ports.

One of the Australian government's main concerns at the time was that if the Australian grains industry couldn't get wheat out of the country before the middle of 1916, the northern hemisphere harvest would flood the market. They feared it would result in a decline in the price the government could receive for selling Australian wheat.

Europe's wheat shortage intensifies

Despite the mid-year northern hemisphere harvest easing global wheat prices, demand remained strong enough to see some of the Russian wheat being moved to northern ports from southern Russia by truck. It was then exported to the UK through the North Sea port of Archangelsk to bypass the Ottoman blockade of the Dardanelles. The trade route was an immensely expensive and incredibly rare journey for wheat to be taken on. A devastating blow to hopeful wheat importers was then struck when news broke in November that the French planned to retreat from their effort to help break through the Dardanelles. Along with the retreat of troops, would be the abandonment of the idea of getting Russian wheat which would have by then accumulated at ports.

Farmer payouts

With the Australian harvest period quickly approaching, the government began explaining how farmers would be compensated. On the basis of fairness, the government mandated that the sale of wheat would need to be done from a centralised government run 'pool'. Wheat grown by farmers would be aggregated (or pooled) by the government and then sold throughout the year either domestically, or via export.

The deal amounted to all farmers receiving the same average price for their grain at the end of the year. The proposed structure of the payments involved farmers receiving an advance of 3s per bushel on their wheat once it was delivered at harvest time. They would then be issued with a certificate of value for up to 3s per bushel. The exact amount paid would be determined by how successful the government pool traders were in selling their wheat to the overseas market in the coming season. The certificate was transferable into a cash payment at the end of the season once the proceeds were realised.

The actual size of the Australian harvest wound up being far larger than expected. With a record area planted and incredibly favourable growing conditions, a monster 5 million tonne wheat crop was harvested that year. This was a gargantuan 74% above the previous record. While a large crop was exactly what the imperial and Australian governments wanted, the sheer and unexpected size of the crop, coupled with challenges getting the crop out of the country, created headaches for a government who guaranteed the purchase of all wheat grown by farmers.

1916 – A gargantuan Australian harvest is too big to handle

As of early 1916, the price of food had gone up by 28% in Australia, 47% in the UK, 83% in Germany and 113% in Austria since the start of the war.[14] Protests were commonplace in Austria. Meanwhile, Britain and

WAR AND WHEAT

Germany, who were both reliant on foreign supplies, were trying to cut off each other's food supply lines at every opportunity. Their hope was that it would speed up the end of the war. Britain was busy enforcing a blockade around Germany and its allies while Germany was building submarines to destroy British supply ships and the blockade.

Russian efforts to build railways through to the northern port of Kola near Finland and Archangelsk were in full swing. It was no easy feat though. Ships were freezing in the White Sea while land routes were suffering similarly extreme challenges. The aim was to make it easier to get more wheat to the French and British markets and not rely on the Black Sea route that was blocked by the Ottomans.

The year started with growing headaches for the Australian government and the companies who were responsible for organising shipping. Due to a growing freight risk from German submarines in the Mediterranean, insurance premiums for passage through the Suez Canal increased by 33% within a couple of months.[15] By this point, the cost of freight from Australia to the UK was almost triple compared to the month prior to the war.

It was almost crop planting time again in Australia, but the backlog of wheat was still nowhere near having been cleared through export channels. In fact, by mid-May 1916 the Australian government still had approximately 3 million tonnes of wheat to ship, and the next harvest was only six months away.

The imperial British government strongly suggested that the Australian government increase freight offers to obtain more freight from overseas vessel owners.

WORLD WAR I – WAR GOES GLOBAL

With the situation becoming more dire by the day and the government becoming visibly more desperate for freight, shippers even more frequently started declining contracts to ship goods into Australia in fear of their vessel being requisitioned. Meanwhile, the remaining ships coming to Australia with goods to offload added a substantial premium to their charges to compensate them for the risks involved.

By late June 1916, the situation had become so problematic that while Australia's Prime Minister was in Europe for strategic talks, he gave the green light to the purchase of 15 freight vessels. The vessels averaged 8,000 tonnes of cargo space each.[16] At the cost of 2 million pounds, it was estimated to be about three times higher than pre-war levels. The price at which the ships were purchased was being presented as a 'favourable' outcome by the government. The fact that the difficulty of obtaining tonnage was likely to get worse was the argument that the government used to sell their decision to the public.

The ships were expected to start loading wheat in August 1916. The biggest problem was that some of the ships were at the time in use for wartime purposes, and their location could not even be divulged. J.M Paxton who was the chairman of the shipping sectional committee of the Sydney chamber of commerce stated that it was a poor decision to purchase the ships. As far as he was concerned, all the government had to do was offer more for freight and the problem would have been solved.

Instead, the government bought ships, many of which were very costly to maintain because their useful lifetime was coming to an end. The way the numbers stacked up was that if all of the vessels were available instantly, they could carry 120,000 tonnes of wheat in one go. The annual freight capacity would only be 360,000 tonnes because it was only feasible for them to do two to three voyages in a year. The bottom line was that annual tonnage was far from sufficient to carry the multi-million tonne export surplus that had piled up across the country.

Seeing how the country was struggling to handle such a large harvest, the government started planning to substantially upgrade the national logistics and storage system for grain. The new bulk handling system would minimize the amount of grain moving from farm to port by truck. Instead, they would focus on constructing a series of large grain storage facilities across the country and rail connecting more rural areas to ports. The benefit would be that grain could move from rural areas to ports faster. During an oversupply, more grain could be stored in storage sites without worrying about rodents and weather damage.

War, deaths, and conscription starts impacting European production

July 1916 was the beginning of a historic spike in wheat prices which would eventually peak in May 1917 at almost 260% above pre-war levels. In August 1916, a combination of plant disease and frost seriously damaged north American wheat crops. The New York Times reported that the cost of foodstuffs in the US rose a staggering 65% compared to the beginning of the war.[17] As with most times when food prices rose, grain merchants and meat packers were being put in the spotlight. Across England, protests were prevalent demanding the government take measures to reduce food prices.

Meanwhile in Russia, the area being planted to wheat, particularly in the south and southwest of the country, was reduced by between 20-70% in some regions.[18] The decline was the result of a substantial reduction in the availability of labour due to conscription, with labour costs up by 300%-500% since the start of the war.[18] The Russian government moved to import agricultural machinery from abroad to limit the impact of the labour shortage. However, availability of machinery overseas was also low due to the reorganisation of manufacturing for war time goods and freight issues. Furthermore, other countries also wanted to use more machinery due to labour shortages. The situation was similar in France where cropping operations were starting to suffer. In addition to the problems mentioned above in relation to Russia, a significant proportion of France was under German occupation and the requirements for importing wheat were starting to escalate.

At the end of August, Romania which was one of the world's largest oil producers and accounted for almost 10% of European wheat production, declared war on Germany. Romanian flags which were rarely seen in Paris during the war, were hung out in honour of Romania ceasing its neutrality. Up to that point in the war, the biggest outlet for neutral Romanian wheat and oil was the German market. Similarly, Romania was one of the few places Germany could secure supplies from since the bulk of its imports had been cut off by the British blockade of continental Europe.

WAR AND WHEAT

Soon after the announcement of Romania joining the war, three German Zeppelins raided Bucharest and set wheat storage facilities on fire. At the time, wheat shortages in Germany were becoming severe, and the crop being harvested was poor due to the limited availability of nitrate which was being redirected to explosives manufacturing. Germany adopted the strategy of seizing as much wheat as possible from occupied territories, including up to 400,000 tonnes from Belgium, which was not only occupied, but also had a population on the brink of starvation.[19] The challenge for Germany was that the war was stretching out and new wheat crops weren't being grown in occupied regions. Farmers in occupied lands had no incentive to continue farming.

Not only did allied countries have an external challenge in obtaining grain via imports, but they also had an internal challenge. Local grain merchants were hesitant to buy and hold large stocks of grain for fear of what would happen to the market price if a glut of wheat was suddenly released from the Black Sea following an allied victory. They were worried that prices would plummet, and they would be left holding a very large loss-making amount of grain. As a consequence, the UK government ruled that it was no longer safe to leave the importation of grain to the private sector where the concern with profits trumped the importance of national security. A royal commission was set up to secure adequate and regular supplies of wheat and flour from overseas. The government would requisition vessels for shipping wheat to the UK and pay a fixed rate to owners in exchange. The private grain trade would continue on a very minimal basis.

WORLD WAR I – WAR GOES GLOBAL

The UK, France and Italy began cooperating on wheat purchases to avoid bidding against one another and having to pay higher prices. The committee met daily in London representing all three countries, and purchased their combined requirements from overseas markets including the US which was still neutral at the time.

The next Australian harvest comes into view

Meanwhile, at the beginning of October 1916, most of the previous season's harvest was still within Australia's borders. As it was unsold, the farmers hadn't been given the remaining portion of their promised wheat payment by the government.

Farmer groups were asking for the government to guarantee an upfront payment which would cover at least the cost of production for the coming harvest. They also wanted the government to promise to purchase the entire national crop again in the following year if they were to be persuaded to plant a big crop next April. Farmers wanted more certainty.

While being committed to getting more wheat shipped from Australia, the UK was experiencing a severe shortage of available freight itself. The government was trying to build new vessels faster than they were being sunk, but as a result of the war, 2,000,000 tonnes of freight had been lost. For you to put that number into perspective, the losses were reportedly equivalent to the size of the combined French, Spanish and Italian mercantile fleets before the war.

By October 20, US wheat prices were trading at the highest level since the US Civil War in the 1860s. Just as social unrest played out in Europe and the UK, protests about high prices started to spring up across cities in the US including New York. While the US wasn't directly involved in the war yet, the high price offered for exports by the war-torn European market drew down on the available domestic supplies. The inevitable consequence was rising domestic food prices.

The fight for Romania

At the end of October, Germany was advancing into Romania. Russia knew that the Germans would be able to prolong the war substantially if they could confiscate Romanian wheat, meat and oil. It was estimated that almost two harvests worth of wheat stocks were available in Romania. Newspaper reports stated that this amount was sufficient to enable Germany to continue fighting for an extra 12 months. In response, Russia began to pour troops into Romania.

As large parts of Romania fell to the Germans, many of the country's oil facilities were set alight by British engineers with the reluctant approval of the Romanian government. The explosions were so severe that they blackened the skies above Bucharest, with some of the explosions going off only minutes before the Germans arrived. Four hundred wells and 70 refineries totalling 800,000 tons of crude oil were destroyed. Newspapers reported that the fires were the largest the European continent had ever seen. The Germans weren't able to restore even a quarter of the previous capacity until the European spring of the following year.

In November, newspaper articles in the UK started discussing further price rises for food, and the likelihood of needing to mix wheat with corn to make bread. Diluting bread quality was something the Germans had already began doing. Meanwhile, labour was running short in the UK, and the associate chambers of agriculture predicted and publicly stated that there would be a disastrous shortage of wheat and other essential foods if UK farms continued to be depleted of skilled labour. At the same time, Germany, which had declining food stocks and no means to import food from overseas, started proposing peace terms. These proposals were rebuffed by the UK, France and Russia.

1916 concluded with the Australian government announcing plans to put a tender process together to decide on a company to build grain elevators around the nation to increase the logistical capacity required to effectively manage wheat production in the years to come.

1917 – Food shortages lead to revolution

Fighting continued to rage across Europe as 1916 flowed into 1917. The masses of refugees fleeing from one nation to another, and the need to feed thousands of Prisoners of War made predicting food requirements increasingly difficult for the allies. Newspapers reported that the allies in Europe could need as much as 12.8 million tonnes of wheat imports to meet their food demands for the year.[20] However, supplies from countries excluding Australia could only meet 8.9 million tonnes. This left the allies in Europe desperately hoping Australia could find sufficient freight services to get critical wheat stocks across to them. Germany was busy doing all it could via naval warfare to sink as many wheat ships heading to the allies as possible. Both sides knew that a

WAR AND WHEAT

lack of food caused food riots, and that food riots lead to revolutions, and that revolutions ended wars.

Greece was yet to make a decision on whether it was joining the war or not. The allies, aware of the German influence in Greece via the pro-German king, blockaded Greek trade until the Greeks made a decision and picked a side. As a token of goodwill, In March 1917 the allies offered Greece all of Cyprus in exchange for joining them, before withdrawing the offer after Greece took too long to decide. Inside Greece, the situation was drifting towards starvation in some parts of the country.

In the Middle East, the British announced the successful takeover of Baghdad which was being used for munitions manufacturing. The takeover demoralised the Ottomans in Constantinople and worsened the domestic atmosphere which was already low due to developing food shortages.

In Austria food shortages were reported as being acute, with increasingly distressing reports of hunger and riots breaking out amongst the lower classes from Vienna to Gratz. In Germany, supplies of wheat, rye, barley, and oats looked more promising as the Germans continued to confiscate stocks from the nations they invaded. The diet of the average German was leaner than it was in pre-war times, and while people weren't happy about it, there were no signs of a revolution brewing.

Meanwhile the US population started questioning their nation's neutrality. Mexico had been offering bases for German submarines to dock at on the Mexican coast since November 1916. And on the first of February in 1917, British intelligence sources reportedly decoded a telegram from the German Secretary of State for Foreign

Affairs to the German Ambassador in Mexico. In it he proposed that if the US were to enter the war, Mexico should align with Germany and annex Texas, New Mexico, and Arizona from the United States.

This letter was published in full in the US press, and the somewhat reluctant-to-go-to-war US population quickly did a U-turn, setting off a nationwide demand for war against Germany. Following the developments in the US, Germany declared unrestricted submarine warfare in the north Atlantic Ocean. This included attacks on merchant and passenger vessels alike.

In March 1917, sheer anger at how the war was being handled and external antagonism combined with a catastrophic food shortage across Russia pushed the country into revolution. The shortage arose due to a combination of poor logistics, reduced planting and a reluctance of farmers to sell their wheat. Czar Nicholas was forced to abdicate from the throne before being assassinated in July of 1918.

US enters the war

In April 1917, the US senate passed President Woodrow Wilson's proposal to declare war on Germany. Other neutrals were also edging towards siding with the allies over the unchecked German submarine warfare. A German submarine had recently sunk a flotilla of seven neutral Dutch cargo ships carrying goods including wheat, followed by the sinking of a Norwegian steamer also carrying wheat.

The food situation in the UK kept worsening and the government asked citizens to grow food in their backyards, and began contemplating an alcohol ban to save grain. Across most northern hemisphere nations, from the US to Germany and even neutral countries like Norway, food shortages continued developing. Following severe drought in north America and reduced ability to produce wheat in Europe, global production was expected to be down a massive 23% in 1917 versus 1916. As a result, in late April 1917, the Chicago wholesale wheat price reached its highest level on record. Prices were an astronomical 235% above pre-war levels.

Toward the end of May 1917, America started dedicating military vessels to protect merchant ships carrying goods to the allies. The reduction in the number of ships lost in submarine warfare that resulted was so sudden and large that the insurance rate for ships going to and from North America to the UK declined by a third. By June the US started sending increasing amounts of grain to Europe, and soon implemented the food control bill which included a drastic amendment. The bill prohibited the manufacture of intoxicants for the duration of the war and penalised food speculation and hoarding with a 2,000 pounds fine and two years imprisonment.

The Shipping problem becomes catastrophic in Australia

For Australia, it wasn't a problem of scarcity, but one of excess. Australia still had 3.5 million tonnes of the previous year's harvest stored away at the beginning of June. Much of the wheat was rotting at ports because the industry only had the capacity to export 70,000 tonnes per month. The most wheat ever exported in a single 12 month period prior to the war was

WORLD WAR I – WAR GOES GLOBAL

1.2 million tonnes. The government even started investigating whether it had the expertise to create a ship manufacturing industry in Australia to rid the country of the wheat oversupply.

At the same time, material shortages in Australia reflected how acute the situation was on the front. In fact, when the Australian Minister for Agriculture sent a request to the Agent-General for galvanised iron to be shipped to NSW for use in the stacking and storing of the next season's wheat harvest to avoid rodent damage, the request was knocked back. The government claimed that it had an overriding responsibility for the protection of troops, maintenance of munition dumps, and other war-related purposes. There was actually so much uncertainty about when the war would finish (and who would win), that the Australian government made it an offence to use galvanised iron for anything unrelated to the war. That included building mouse proof fencing around wheat stacks despite the fact that there was a mouse plague at the time.

In late June, the US set up a council to supervise the task of providing food for the allies, and asked neutral nations to provide assistance in shipping the accumulated Australian wheat to Europe. The US was arranging for British dominion wheat to be sent early to conserve the American supply in case it was needed later.

The US government also implemented laws aimed at the export of foodstuffs heading for Holland, Scandinavia, and Switzerland. The US wanted to limit exports to the absolute necessities to ensure as little as possible was able to be sent onward to Germany. The export to neutrals of pig-iron and sulphur was banned. Importantly, the legislature restricted neutral nations the privilege of trading with the allies unless they purchased 100% of their supplies from the allies, thus dismantling their argument that it was necessary to exchange foodstuffs with Germany in order to obtain other vital supplies.

The northern hemisphere suffers through pre-harvest food shortages

In Europe, supplies were running dangerously low in the last month before mid-year harvest as labour shortages continued to grow.

In the UK, out of the total of almost 1.3 million people engaged in agriculture before the war, 678,000 had been called to arms so far. Wheat acreage in the UK shrunk 12% in late 1916 compared to the year prior, and in France by 21%.[21,23] Newspapers stated that shortages in Europe were getting worse and it would now need to import an estimated 15.5 million tonnes of wheat in the coming season. Whereas the exportable wheat of the allies was expected to be only 10.1 million tonnes. Argentina was becoming increasingly dry while the US was about to harvest its smallest number of winter wheat hectares in 40 years due to drought.

Meanwhile, Germany stationed a large fleet of submarines in the Azores, a group of Portuguese islands between Europe and the US, in an attempt to separate United States food and military supplies from Europe.

Telling farmers to stop farming was not an option

In late July, the expansion of the Australian grain handling system was finally given the green light by the government. The plan was for a number of sheds

WORLD WAR I – WAR GOES GLOBAL

that already existed on country railway stations to be transformed into large scale storage facilities by January 1918. The government knew that it would be catastrophic if there was nowhere to store another large wheat harvest because the previous one was still stuck in storage sites across the country. The commission looking into how much grain a well-designed bulk handling scheme could handle found that working capacity and silo capacity needed to be equivalent to one third of the crop for which the scheme was designed. They were aware that the one-third of an average crop rule would not cover the current emergency situation of record sized crops, but that it would be suitable after the war when production would in theory come down.

The Commonwealth government advanced nearly 3 million pounds to state governments who would be responsible for repaying it over ten years by way of an annual payment made through charging fees for the storage of farmer's grain. The NSW government announced that 71 emergency grain silos in the state's wheat districts would be built to avoid all of the soon to be harvested wheat from spoiling in fields.

The alternative to improving the industry's infrastructure to store and move grain would be telling some farmers to stop farming to ease the surplus. The result would be leaving farm workers unemployed, farms without an income and putting the country at risk of severe shortages during a future drought. If farmers were told to farm less, some may have permanently moved out of rural communities, hobbling the farming sector for many years even after the war finished. An industry can be shrunken quickly, but it takes a very long time to build it back up.

WAR AND WHEAT

Meanwhile, with the price of petrol in Australia having doubled compared to pre-war levels, and with the possibility of future shortages becoming very realistic, the federal government started debating whether to create a power-alcohol industry which could convert crops into transport fuel.[22] The creation of a power-alcohol industry would reduce the country's reliance on the importation of fossil fuels. For simplicity we will refer to power-alcohol as 'biofuel' moving forward.

Allies ramp up effort while Germany shows early signs of weakness

In order to conserve enough wheat for home and allied use, the US food administrator issued a warning that US wheat consumption had to fall by 30%. Over in the UK, ship building activity had been ramped up to three times the pace of productive pre-war years. Even with the increase in production, only 1.6 million tonnes of shipping freight was created in 1917, while 0.5 million tonnes was being sunk by German U-boats each month.[23]

In Germany, munitions factories were reducing working hours due to a shortage of indispensable metals. Sickness and malnutrition were rife amongst the population. The bread people were eating was infected with hay and potato bacteria. There simply wasn't enough wheat to make bread that was fit for consumption. What made the situation increasingly dire in Germany was that the just harvested wheat yields were estimated to be 40% below normal.

With food availability quickly shrinking and the population growing increasingly dissatisfied with how the war was being handled, the German government started proposing peace talks again. They were even willing to hand over Belgium to the Belgians if they would untangle their allegiance with the allies and become neutral. Germany demanded that the English and French monopoly of the Mediterranean would have to cease as part of any peace deal. Austria was willing to negotiate for an 'honourable' peace. Sensing weakness and not prepared to allow Germany to hold onto its gains, the allies rebuffed the offer. The allies were making significant progress in the Balkans with plans to advance into Bulgaria and cut off Germany from supplies in Turkey. The objective was to neutralise Bulgaria and force upon Turkey a separate peace from that being planned for Germany.

1918 – moving into the last stage of WWI

The beginning of 1918 was marked by more rioting across Europe, with anger even breaking out in the UK. Food wholesalers were allowed to purchase government butter reserves and then resell them in regions with shortages. Regions from which the butter was being moved thought that the wholesalers were going to simply hoard it from the public and sell it later at a higher price.

In Russia, the collective energy of the country was paralysed by the revolution. Germany sensed weakness and opportunistically moved in to make a bilateral peace with Russia with the intention of keeping all of the Russian areas it had conquered, in addition to having control over Russia's wheat supplies. Negotiations were made difficult by the factions inside the new Russian

WAR AND WHEAT

government. By February, Russia made it clear that it would no longer participate in the war. By March, both militarily and politically exhausted, Ukrainians and Russians entered into a peace with Germany. The treaty that was entered into gave Germany and Austria access to the remaining Ukrainian wheat reserves. Around the same time news began seeping out of Russia that the large stocks of wheat that were spread across the country (including in Ukraine), had either already been consumed, or they were simply rotting away. The revelation came as a blow to the Germans who were hoping to resupply their food stockpiles.

Meanwhile, the US government was focusing on building more vessels than the total of the allied ones being sunk by the Germans each week. The US plan was to construct around 6 million tonnes of cargo space a year. The plan was expected to employ half a million men and use the equivalent of around 15% of the steel being produced in the US annually.

In May, the US War Trade Board allocated US ships to take Australian wheat to the west coast of America. The inflow of Australian wheat to the west coast would allow US and Canadian wheat to move from the US east coast toward Europe without worries of domestic shortages arising. This was more advantageous than moving Australian wheat directly to Europe because it avoided the threat of German U boats in the Mediterranean and security risks around the Suez Canal. Furthermore, the US was not willing to protect foreign vessels heading to Europe, only American ones.

The deployment of US troops in Europe resulted in a visible turning of the tide. The deployment forced

Germany to spread its military thinner across more fronts. With US troops deployed in Western Europe, Germany and Austria had to divert more troops from other fronts. However, the Austrians refused to send troops west in case Italy attacked them from the south. Similarly, the German military leaders stationed in the east claimed that if they were sent west, they wouldn't be able to protect their claims on Ukrainian and Russian wheat supplies in occupied areas. Germany desperately needed the supplies to avoid internal turmoil at home. Furthermore, the Germans feared that even if the Russians didn't take back occupied territories with wheat stocks, the now desperate Austrians would take the wheat. At this point, the Austrians were even closer to starvation than the Germans were.

Tide turns further in allied favour

By July 1918, food supplies in allied countries, particularly in Britain, improved dramatically. In the UK, more favourable seasonal conditions saw crop production improve, while the protection of vessels by the American navy allowed imports to come into port without the kind of cargo losses experienced earlier in the war.

By August, Germany was very visibly starting to lose ground and retreat. Battles were being lost and allies were taking tens of thousands of German soldiers as Prisoners of War. Meanwhile Russia was in the midst of constant internal turmoil between the red-Bolsheviks and the anti-Bolshevik White army that was supported by the allies. Concerned that the allies wanted a counterrevolution, on the 12th of August Lenin even stated that there was a state of war between Russia and the allies. This followed the deployment of allied troops in northern Russia, and Japanese troops in eastern Russia.

By October, peasant revolts started to break out in the Ukraine and threatened German occupation, including their access to local wheat supplies. Meanwhile Germany's loss of occupied lands and battles to the British, Americans and French accelerated. Eventually Germany and Austria together sent a peace note to the US president asking for an armistice. The note was strongly rebuffed. The US president demanded unconditional surrender, an end to autocracy in Germany, and the forfeiting of the entire German shipping fleet to the allies. The plan was for the German fleet to be distributed according to the losses inflicted by Germany. The allied powers wanted to permanently disarm and dismantle Germany's ability to wage war.

By mid-October, German newspapers started to clearly state for the first time that Germany was losing multiple battles and that troops were being pushed back. With that, the internal blame game began. The Social Democrats were holding meetings across Germany demanding the country be turned into a republic.

November 1918 – the war ends!

On the 11th of November, Germany officially surrendered to the allies. While an armistice was reached, a peace deal was not yet signed. Hence military readiness and government controls over the economy hadn't been curtailed yet in Europe. Shipping was still being constrained by governments, but freight rates to the UK from Australia on the private market had already fallen considerably.

Allied governments began rushing to feed millions of starving citizens in previously occupied regions to minimise the chance of a revolution. The threat of revolution was constantly brewing, particularly when it came to the communists. Protests and food riots were already breaking out in Holland. While the war had ended; people were still starving.

Meanwhile, to safeguard the success of the US grains industry in the post war phase, the US embargoed all wheat imports. This included Australian wheat, but excluded wheat that was already on the water in transit. Like Australia, the US had incentivised farmers to grow as much wheat as possible during the war. Now that the war was over, fears of prices plummeting resulted in the government restricting imports of wheat to ensure domestic prices didn't drop too far.

Australia, with its large wheat supplies and dramatically improved ability to ship wheat was in an ideal position to take advantage of the post-war environment. The Prime Minister of Australia went into negotiations to sell one million tonnes of wheat reserves to the UK. The government and grains industry proposed to the imperial government that if they sold it 1 million tonnes of wheat at a reasonable price, future harvests could be allowed to be sold to wherever the Australian Wheat Board chose. The final price offered by the British was below expectations. However, with farmers in need of cash, the government accepted the offer.

Extra shipping supplies began rapidly arriving on the global stage as Germany surrendered its entire

WAR AND WHEAT

navy to the allies. Germany's colonies were being divided amongst the victors - primarily the UK and the US. The Australian government requested from the UK that Nauru was handed over to them. Nauru would provide phosphate reserves that could be used as fertiliser on Australian wheat fields. Furthermore, the transfer of ownership would ensure that Germany would be deprived of the use of phosphate for explosives production in any future wars.

Following the end of WWI, the Russian agricultural system fell into disrepair. With insufficient volumes of food being produced to feed its own people, the country saw mass starvation, particularly in present day Ukraine. The need to feed millions of starving Europeans kept global wheat prices high in the years immediately following WWI.

CHAPTER TWO

World War II – The Curse of Australia is Procrastination

> *"The curse of Australia is procrastination. We debate things in parliament eternally, but we hardly ever do anything." "I am afraid the awakening will be a rude one."*
> J.M Harcourt January 1st 1938,
> Sydney Morning Herald.

The potential for war, destruction, and death once again started to rear its ugly head above the horizon in early 1938, more than a year prior to WWII officially beginning.

Between the end of WWI and the beginning of WWII, the Australian population grew from 5.1 million to 7 million people. Australia was still a very sparsely populated and young nation.

Local commentators were writing about signs of a new world war brewing, and demanding that Australia develop its resources and itself as a nation. The country was slow to develop local industries which could make it both more self-sufficient, and able to support allies in future conflicts. Not only that, but it was also slow to stop sending critical raw materials to future foes.

WAR AND WHEAT

Since Japan invaded China in 1937, there had been no measurable response from Australia. In fact, trade with Japan rose despite various proposals for a boycott. The value of exports to Japan for the preceding 6 months to January 1938 totalled 2 million pounds versus 0.431 million pounds a year prior.

Meanwhile, the global wheat glut had depressed wheat prices and squeezed the profit margins of Australian farmers. To help growers, the Australian government even contemplated implementing a new tax on flour millers, and using the funds to subsidise farmers. Flour millers were making large profits because their input cost for producing flour (i.e. wheat) had declined, but the cost of flour and bread remained stable.

One year and nine months before WWII began

January 1938 began with Germany demanding either the return of its colonies that were taken as part of its defeat in WWI, or an easing of war reparations. The western world firmly refused. Meanwhile, Spain was in the grips of a civil war between the republicans and nationalists. The republican side was being supported by the west and Russia, while the nationalists were being supported by Nazi Germany and Italy. Poverty and anger across Europe were still rife following the mass loss of life, the need to make reparation payments to the victors, and the division of land after WWI. In Hungary, flags permanently flew at half-mast in mourning for the nation's lost provinces. The loss was something Hungarians were adamant not to forget. In primary schools, children were taught songs that

WORLD WAR II – THE CURSE OF AUSTRALIA IS PROCRASTINATION

lamented the lost provinces, vowing that at the proper time each child would do all that was in his or her power to get the provinces back.

Nationalism was roaring back to life across central Europe. With apparent disregard to the economic viability of the goal, almost every country was seeking to make itself more self-sufficient and independent from the rest of the world, including in wheat production.

Economic activity around the world started finally recovering following the boom-and-bust environment that had been in place since the end of WWI. However, the feeling of buoyancy had more to do with billions of dollars being spent on re-armament rather than the thriving of normal productive industries. On the 1st of January 1938, a commentator from the Argus newspaper by the name of J.P Jones MLC asked what would happen when it "became no longer practicable to spend more money on machines of destruction. What would the men and women do when thrown in the labour market? The world will be faced with the choice of using its enormous store of armaments or sinking into a depression worse than the one following WWI".

European stockpiling begins

In early February 1938, the British parliament started discussing the stockpiling of food. Britain was reportedly only a quarter self-sufficient in its ability to feed a population that was four million people larger than it was at the beginning of WWI.[24] Not only were there more people to feed, but shipping capacity had shrunk, thereby limiting Britain's ability to import enough food in the event of a war breaking out.

WAR AND WHEAT

Parliamentarians were advocating for the government to store a years' worth of food supplies. Only three days after the UK started conversations around stockpiling, the Greek government permitted the importation of Australian wheat, and a fleet of 20 Greek vessels were chartered to load grain that had been harvested in Western Australia. Whether the strategy that was employed by the Greeks was related to the fear of another war isn't clear. However, in light of the acute food shortages Greece suffered during WWI, it's likely that the government had no interest in taking any chances.

Beginning of aggression and acceleration of German strategic planning

In late February 1938, Hitler sent German troops into Austria and forced the Austrian chancellor to accept far-reaching demands. Commentators in Australia were writing that it was not a victory for peaceful settlement in Europe, but a victory for gangsterism. The annexation triggered a rush of gold hoarding by governments across the European continent. Not long after, the value of Czechoslovakian bonds begun to tank as concerns about the Czechs being next on Germany's hit list mounted. Over in Britain, talk of rapid rearmament started becoming frequent and prominent on front page news.

Meanwhile, as Germany was threatening Austria, Australia was still willingly selling the Germans significant volumes of raw materials. For example, exports of wool to Germany in the last half of 1937 totalled 96,614 bales, compared to 73,033 in the same

WORLD WAR II – THE CURSE OF AUSTRALIA IS PROCRASTINATION

period of the previous year, and 54,520 bales in 1935. The textiles industry in Germany was in overdrive, with many factories working at double their normal shift rates, presumably preparing military orders. In February, Germany had also begun sweeping up and purchasing wheat from a variety of odd and uncommon ports, including 50,000 tonnes from Egypt.

By taking Austria, Germany was able to surround Czechoslovakia from the west. They wanted Czechoslovakia's chrome and wheat reserves, as well as the ability to carve out a corridor to Hungary and Romania to ensure Germany had access to a vast source of oil and additional wheat reserves. Romania at the time had fascist groups waiting to seize the government with Germany's support. The Romanians produced 8 million tonnes of crude oil every year, and if Germany could absorb it entirely, there would be little need to expensively synthesis oil out of coal.

At this point, Germany was only halfway through Goering's four-year plan to regiment every aspect of economic life to make Germany independent of foreign raw materials. The German's were well aware that it takes self-sufficiency in food and energy production to win a long-drawn-out war from their experience in WWI.

Germany's economic planners had urged the government for years to win over central Europe politically. However, resentment against Germany from the first world war was hard to overcome. The feeling of antipathy changed once economic recession in central Europe started being felt from 1937, and prices of commodities including wheat and oil declined sharply. At the time, Romanian wheat was laying in fields rotting while waiting for a buyer.

WAR AND WHEAT

The UK starts purchasing large wheat cargoes

With the geopolitical trajectory becoming clearer by the day, there was renewed strategic discussion between soon to be allies around food and raw materials procurement coordination.

In early April 1938, British millers began purchasing Australian wheat cargoes without the usual intensive bargaining. Prices for wheat inside the UK rose quickly and considerably. The UK government started developing policies for food rationing and distribution that could be put into effect as soon as a war started. Immediately upon the outbreak of war an order would be issued requisitioning all stocks of cereals and cereal products in the country. The only exceptions were deliveries relating to existing contracts in quantities required for normal consumption. No room would be left for speculative or profiteering purposes.

From that time onwards, the supply and distribution of cereals was going to be overseen by the trade industry acting as agents for the government. Area Grain Committees would be setup for the handling, storing, and despatching of supplies arriving. There was also a number of shadow committees that would be ready to step in at short notice in the event of the other committees being incapacitated due to the war. On the Axis-side, Italy moved to ban flour exports while continuing to import wheat.

Dealing with a surplus was not just an Australian problem

The wheat farming world experienced a severe economic contraction following WWI, especially from 1928 to 1933. A string of good production

WORLD WAR II – THE CURSE OF AUSTRALIA IS PROCRASTINATION

seasons globally coincided with the great economic depression. Consumption was declining while overproduced grain was piling up in major producing regions. The oversupply was exaggerated by the earlier mentioned drive for self-sufficiency. Germany, Italy, and France who typically imported wheat in large quantities prior to WWI, had set up major policies to ensure they were as self-sufficient as possible in case of another war. Through subsidies for grain farmers and an increased consumption of rye, these countries gradually lessened their wheat imports. By 1934 they were almost entirely self-sufficient.

By mid-1938, France was facing an overwhelming surplus following a second consecutive record wheat harvest. Despite the excess wheat reserves, the French government kept the local price artificially high to appease farmers. The government decided to deal with part of the surplus by distilling the wheat into alcohol for use in car engines as a fuel, with the balance being bought by the military for national security purposes. The cost of dealing with the surplus to taxpayers was considerable. While exporting the surplus may seem to be the obvious solution to a surplus, the price offered overseas was below the cost of production in France at the time.

Germany gears up for war

In mid-August 1938, Germany was performing military manoeuvres and continued to stock up its supplies of wheat. Flour mills were told to have two months of reserves stored up. The German public were becoming increasingly alarmed by the rising number of military manoeuvres taking place inside the country. Meanwhile, tractors started pulling anti-aircraft guns through the streets in Britain.

In early September, Britain and America moved towards signing a free trade agreement to remove trade barriers for wheat. Meanwhile, both Italy and Germany had harvested wheat crops that were below their minimum requirements. On the other hand, Balkan production was very strong and provided a large surplus that both nations planned to tap into for their stockpiling requirements. At the same time, Germany was rumoured to be constructing a widescale system of grain storage sites across the country in order to store grain for longer periods.

The private sector is on edge

With a full year to go until Germany invaded Poland, insurance companies were becoming increasingly hesitant to provide shipping insurance to the private sector. Scarred by their experience in WWI, private sector British underwriters simply weren't prepared to undertake the risks inherent in a future war. The lack of insurance quickly placed impediments on grain buyers looking to import into the UK. The trading of wheat futures in London and Liverpool temporarily all but ceased.

A group representing the shipping industry urged the government to immediately adopt a system of state insurance against war risks. They stated that without such a system, the ability of the private sector to build up reserves of foodstuffs and other essential commodities would be significantly impacted. The British government responded to those concerns by

WORLD WAR II – THE CURSE OF AUSTRALIA IS PROCRASTINATION

stating that they had a system ready, but it would only be implemented in the case of an emergency.

Last attempts to avert war – the Munich Agreement

On the 24th of September 1938, Hitler issued the Godesberg Memorandum to Czechoslovakia. Hitler was demanding that Czechoslovakia cede the Sudetenland to Nazi Germany following a plebiscite vote to be taken on the 31st of October. Under the agreement, German soldiers would be allowed in the area being voted on while the vote was ongoing. On September 28th the Czechs rejected the memorandum. Meanwhile, France ordered the mobilisation of 600,000 men, and the Royal British Navy mobilised their troops in concert.

In an attempt to avert a broader war, the Munich Agreement was signed in the last days of September. The agreement stated that Czechoslovakia had to surrender its border region (the Sudetenland) to Nazi Germany and was signed by Great Britain, France, Germany and Italy.

Democracies and Germany vie for economic and political influence in central Europe

In November of 1938, the western nations and the Germans were actively trying to provide economic assistance to central Europe. They were both trying to loan money to Bulgaria and Romania in order to receive monopolies on their exports of commodities. The UK parliament began discussing a possible Anglo-French joint initiative around providing economic assistance to Romania, Czechoslovakia, and Yugoslavia. The purpose was to enable those countries to resist German

WAR AND WHEAT

pressure and be less dependent on the German market economically, especially when it came to the sale of wheat, petrol, and other raw materials.

Not long after this plan was put forward, Britain purchased 200,000 tonnes of Romanian wheat to be stored by the food defence department as an addition to the nation's war reserves that already exceeded 750,000 tonnes at the time. [25] With this result, the British government announced that their food supplies were coming close to a years' worth of consumption. However, John Maynard Keynes was of the view that more food needed to be stored, and the government should pay to store it. The private sector had no economic incentive to buy and store large tonnages of wheat. Storing grain costs money, both directly and via the opportunity cost in terms of what that money could be used for elsewhere.

The Germans were actively negotiating with Romania to hand over their undeveloped oil reserves in exchange for Germany purchasing a large range and volume of Romania's raw materials, thus supporting them economically. Germany also started selling arms to the Hungarians in exchange for their produce. It may at first appear odd that Germany needed to convince other countries to join its supply chain as opposed to just invading and taking what they wanted. However, it must be remembered that when Germany invaded Romania in WWI, Romania set almost all of its own oil and some of its food reserves on fire on the way out.

Hermann Goering stated that Germany had two years' worth of wheat supplies as they continued to import more. 250,000 tonnes were imported in the month of October alone. Germany wasn't willing to make the same mistake they made in WWI when they started running short on food. In that case they had to divert troops to eastern Europe to shore up food supplies, leaving defence lines vulnerable.

By the end of November, Romanian powerbrokers told the British that they either needed to purchase significantly more of its exports than they already had, or (at least from an economic and trade standpoint) they had no choice but to move closer to the German camp.

Australia readies for war

Opinion pieces in Australian newspapers advocated the re-establishment of a series of area offices to register men between the age of 18 and 50 who had the capacity to either work or fight. At the time, Australia only had 35 thousand volunteers. According to newspapers, most of those men only had access to an inadequate ten days of training every year.

There was a flash point in December 1938 when Port Kembla workers in New South Wales refused to load pig iron onto a vessel bound for Japan. Prime Minister Menzies came out publicly to lambast the protest, stating that Australia would not allow groups of people to dictate the nation's foreign policy. Menzies claimed that meddling directly in trade would only increase the risk of international strife. At this point, Australia's leaders were (incorrectly) of the view that Japan's ambitions could be satiated solely by its invasion of China.

Meanwhile, the grains industry was busy dealing with low wheat prices. Low prices combined with news that the British government was actively preparing the nation for war prompted the Australian Wheat Grower's Federation to request the Australian government set a minimum wheat price. It also wanted a re-establishment of an export control board to organise the bulk purchase of Australian wheat by the British government. The plan was again to create a centralised national board to control the chartering, selling, financing, and allocating of overseas sales between the states. Meanwhile the state boards would deal with domestic affairs such as the handling of grain movements and sales within the state.

Following the unsuccessful creation of a biofuel industry in WWI, talk of creating the industry rose to the surface again. The purpose being argued related to making use of the grain that couldn't be exported due to freight shortages, and securing fuel supplies for the military and economy.

At the time, grain merchants were busy selling wheat to India until December 1938. The Indian government introduced an import tax on wheat to reduce cheap imports dragging down local prices and the profit margins Indian farmers received. The government wanted to avoid local production declining. With war on the horizon, and the legacy of catastrophic shortages experienced during WWI still fresh in the minds of decision makers, the last thing any government wanted was to jeopardise the domestic production of wheat. The objective of a domestic wheat industry in any country isn't simply to make money, it also exists for the purpose of national survival during times of crisis when the ability to import food is curtailed.

1939 – the year the world unravelled

Commodity and financial markets were unusually quiet at the beginning of the year, especially considering the unfolding geopolitical environment. It was the quite before the storm. The UK was busy finishing building shelters against gas attacks, while Japan constructed electric wiring around French and British settlements in Shanghai.

In early March, Germany and Romania signed an agreement which would allow the Germans to develop Romania's agricultural, petroleum, shipping, banking and armaments industries. Under the agreement 90% of Romania's wheat harvest would now go to Germany. In effect, Romania would become a branch factory servicing the needs of the Germans. By this time German experts had already been working for months to reorganise Romania's railway administration. Now Germany would go onto supervise the whole of Romanian land, sea and air traffic.

On March 15th, German troops faced limited resistance when they invaded what remained of Czechoslovakia. They instantly began the confiscation of government commodity reserves, including wheat, and the deportation of the Jewish population.

Dealing with a world awash with wheat

By April, the world had become awash with wheat. Global production was up by over 8 million tonnes versus the year prior, and global trade rose to the highest level in decades. The World Wheat Advisory Committee met in London to discuss the global wheat surplus. Most of the largest wheat-producing countries in the world were members of the committee which came out of the International Wheat Agreement of 1933. The aim of the agreement was to stabilise price fluctuations in the international wheat markets. It was all about avoiding the kind of boom to bust cycle the agricultural industries experienced during and immediately after WWI.

There were three primary drivers that resulted in the oversupply. First, wheat planting acreage increased substantially in non-European countries during and after WWI. The countries in question included Argentina, Australia, the United States, and Canada.

Second, there was a long-awaited post-war recovery in production in the European Danuban basin. The first world war significantly disrupted the ability of countries in the area to produce agricultural goods. The four main Danuban countries saw exports decline from 4.4 million tonnes annually prior to WWI, to a mere 1.4 million tonnes in the year following the end of WWI.

Third, Germany, Italy and France reduced their import requirements substantially as they moved towards self-sufficiency. Due to the amount of disruption and pain caused by food shortages experienced during WWI, governments were determined to keep domestic production high despite concerns around surpluses being experienced from time to time.

There had previously never been a long-range plan from a global, or even an individual nation's perspective, to balance supply and demand during an enormous global oversupply. Many nation's governments feared that if they were to forcefully reduce planted hectares, it could coincide with a drought, in which case production could collapse. The worst-case scenario would be experienced if this occurred in the lead up to or during a conflict.

In Australia, the federal government began actively discussing strategies to control the storage and shipment of wheat in a national emergency. The aim of organising the industry was to first ensure an adequate supply of wheat was available to all vital demand centres in Australia. And second, to provide proper storage to ensure that wheat surpluses could be kept from rotting until shipping availability arose.

Germany asks trading partners to trade in German currency instead of British Pounds

Due to a lack of foreign currency reserves, Germany began using a barter system to gain influence in central Europe and obtain the resources like oil and wheat that it needed. The Germans did not pay for goods in foreign currency, but gave trade counterparts German credits that could be used to purchase German goods. With time, Germany limited which German goods could be exchanged for the credits.

The Germans eventually ruled out providing any goods in exchange for the credit that could easily be sold on international markets for foreign currencies like British pounds or US dollars. For example, Germany allowed useless German typewriters and calculators to be exchanged for credits. The further into the trade relationship Germany and another country got, and the more German credits the other country accumulated, the more Germany constrained what could be purchased. If the other country grew dissatisfied, Germany simply said "fine, then your credits become worthless".

The allies also started to move away from trading in currencies. The US and European countries adopted a barter system to avoid causing significant

WAR AND WHEAT

volatility in their currencies. Government-to-government transactions were becoming immensely large and increasingly frequent. The US made plans to exchange cotton and wheat for rubber and tin. The objective was to not only stockpile the commodities it lacked, but also to gain political influence in south America and parts of Europe. The exchange worked particularly well for the United States because it did not produce enough tin or rubber itself, and was anxious to dispose of their uncomfortably large surplus of cotton and wheat.

The British were increasingly having their needs met by US produced wheat and cotton. The complaints of Australian and Canadian traders who had previously provided those commodities to the UK fell on deaf ears. The US comforted the two nations by stating that imports of US wheat and cotton would stay in UK government reserves for at least five years before entering the market if they were unused. Traders said that large quantities of a commodity, even if it was inside government storage, would weigh on any price upside. Interestingly, from a strategic perspective, it would have made more sense to stock up on Australian wheat first instead of American supplies, because it would be more difficult to import materials all the way from Australia if a war began.

In the following months, more barter systems would be put in place, including an arrangement being set up between Britain and the USSR. That move would undoubtably have angered the Germans who were close to signing a non-aggression pact with the Soviet Union.

WORLD WAR II – THE CURSE OF AUSTRALIA IS PROCRASTINATION

An Anglo-Turkish alliance to keep the Black Sea open in case of war

In early June 1939, Britain and Turkey signed an agreement to keep the Black Sea open for the allies in the event of a war. After losing in WWI, and in moral opposition to the Italians after they attacked Turkish Libya in 1911, Turkey was willing to sign the agreement that would hinder the aims of the Axis Alliance which included Italy. The arrangement would allow Britain and France to fulfil guarantees they made to Romania against aggression by Nazidom by allowing British warships, and, if necessary, French and British troops to access the Black Sea. Furthermore, the wheat trade from southern Russia to the allies and the munitions/materials needed for Russia from the west could continue to move through the canal during a war.

On the 23rd of August 1939, Germany's Foreign minister Joachim von Ribbentrop visited Moscow and signed a non-aggression agreement with Stalin. The two countries agreed to not take any military action against one another for ten years. That included during, or in response to, Germany's impending invasion of Poland.

On the brink of war

Two days later, on Friday the 25th of August, Australian newspapers reported that politicians left parliament in Canberra with the feeling that hope of avoiding conflict was slender. The view was that war would unfold even before the weekend began. The cabinet arranged for all preparations to be completed to place

WAR AND WHEAT

Australia on a war footing if it was necessary. The ministry discussed economic measures to co-operate with the British in the event of war breaking out. This included a general embargo being placed on the export of materials to the belligerents.

Meanwhile, the world awaited Japan's reaction after Germany and Russia signed the non-aggression pact. At the time, the Japanese were on Germany's side in theory. However, they had officially been in a state of war with Russia since the war of 1904-05 where Japan became the first Asian power to win against a European power in modern times.

Germany shows signs it is prepared to move forward

In the last days of August 1939, Germany started distributing ration cards to citizens covering foodstuffs, soap, coal, boots and shoes, as well as calling up all reservists. German newspapers announced that it had 8.5 million tonnes of wheat in reserve, claiming that it would be enough for at least a year. All railways were instantly reserved for government use, and German merchant ships were recalled to home ports. Air services were also suspended and rail services between Germany and Denmark were cancelled. The German-Dutch border was also closed to prevent military desertion.

At the same time, the US sent additional troops and anti-aircraft and coastal guns to the Panama Canal to ensure key trade routes remained open for itself and its allies. By this time, the UK had filled their granaries up to capacity, and they were buying Canadian wheat and storing it in Canada for future shipment, if and when it was needed.

WORLD WAR II – THE CURSE OF AUSTRALIA IS PROCRASTINATION

World War II officially begins

On the 1st of September, Germany invaded Poland. Britain soon after declared war on Germany and WW2 began. On the 17th of September, Russia also moved into Poland.

In Australia, the pre-planned steps for the agricultural industry in the case of war were instantly executed. In the first week of the war, the British government bought the entire Australian wool clip, and the Federal government started the procedure of nationalising the Australian grains industry once again. A committee was created by the Commonwealth to control the wheat harvest through a pooling of resources. The Commonwealth immediately acquired ownership (on paper) of all of the wheat in Australia at the time, with the exception of the wheat that was owned by farmers and stored on farms. The overarching approach was aimed at having as much centralisation as possible to enable cohesion in decision making.

An advisory committee consisting of millers, merchants, wheat pooling authorities, growers and those involved in grain logistics was set up in each state to supervise the general operations of the industry under the supervision of a commonwealth board. In the same way as things were handled in WWI, existing grain traders and grain handling companies were appointed as agents for the Commonwealth. They had responsibility for collecting, handling and storing the harvested wheat.

The intention was for the board to be able to sell wheat at the most opportune price because of the leveraging power they had when negotiating with other governments for a good price and for shipment space. The returns would then be distributed among the growers according to the tonnage they had produced.

WAR AND WHEAT

As it did in WWI, the government began contemplating whether and when to cancel all recent contracts between grain merchants and farmers. This would impact grain merchants who had contracts to buy wheat from farmers at the low price they agreed to before the war.

Allied nations empty the Romanian wheat pantry

Between the start and the middle of September, Romanian wheat prices rocketed up 30% and barley prices rose 100% as British, French, and Dutch merchants purchased any remaining stock before it was snapped up by others.[26] The logic behind the large purchases was two-fold. First, it was a last-ditch attempt to convince Romania to shift its allegiance to the allied side. Second, it was an equally important opportunity to leave as little stock as possible for Germany to be able to purchase or take forcefully at a later date.

Germany was demanding Yugoslavia deliver wheat that it had purchased. Yugoslavia was refusing. The Yugoslavian government was demanding that Germany first send back 400 rail trucks and 100 river barges from previous shipments. Meanwhile, over in Italy, special military squads were set up around food stores to avoid hoarding. Any shopkeepers who were caught hoarding were arrested. Harking back to the experience of WWI, submarine warfare was instantly up and running.

Russia-Germany tensions rise

Towards the end of 1939, Russia was forcing Germany to pull back their activity in Poland and leave more area for them to take over. Remember, at

WORLD WAR II – THE CURSE OF AUSTRALIA IS PROCRASTINATION

this time, Germany and Russia were the signatories of a non-aggression pact. Meanwhile, the German manufacturing sector became increasingly concerned that if Germany gave Russia more of Poland, they would not have the raw materials necessary to produce the needed tradable goods. These goods were needed so they could be sold to pay for imports from southeast Europe – primarily oil and wheat. While the initial arrangement was for eastern European countries to receive German credits instead of hard currency as payment for exports, eventually exporting countries lost interest in the scheme.

Meanwhile across the Atlantic, Mexico threatened to confiscate ten German ships that were currently docked in Mexico's harbours if Germany failed to pay its oil debt. And Romania began refusing to deliver oil and grain to Germany until an outstanding trade balance had been settled. Also, Russia made an agreement with Bulgaria for all commodity exports to go to them, rather than two thirds of them going to Germany which was previously the case. Russia's pivot to eastern and southern Europe meant that Hungary, Italy, Romania, Yugoslavia, Greece, Turkey, and Bulgaria had a new major outlet for their produce and oil apart from Germany.

The US attempts to coax South America into staying out of the war

The US held a conference in Panama for all 21 South American Republics on the 3rd of October 1939. The main goal of the conference was to create a common neutrality policy to keep South America out of the war

WAR AND WHEAT

to avoid hostilities flaring up between countries in the United States' neighbourhood. The secondary purpose was to redirect the trade that was in place with countries in Europe towards more inter-American (north/south) trade. The aim of this strategy was to minimise economic losses that would be born in the event of the US being cut off from European markets.

Furthermore, South America produced a broad spectrum of goods that were necessary for war. These included meat and wheat for human consumption, and the nitrates that Germany needed for fertiliser. The US was hoping to cut off these supplies to the Axis powers of Germany, Italy and Japan from the onset of the war. The US also wanted to include a demand that compelled all republics to refuse belligerent warships entry into their ports. The only countries that were not willing to comply at the time were Uruguay and Argentina. In fact, the relationship between the US and Argentina turned increasingly negative as the war progressed.

In November, Britain and the USSR signed a deal to exchange Russian timber for UK tin and rubber, and Russian wheat for British machinery. While it was stressed that this was a purely economic transaction, the Germans (with whom the Russians had a non-aggression pact) were unlikely to have seen it that way.

Meanwhile the wheat trade supplying the allies and the Axis members continued. Despite German submarines sinking neutral ships, European countries on the allied side were receiving nearly as much wheat as they were before the outbreak of the war. Exports of grain from Romania, Bulgaria and Yugoslavia to Germany had also increased above pre-war levels.

WORLD WAR II – THE CURSE OF AUSTRALIA IS PROCRASTINATION

The US begins supporting the allied war effort

On the 31st of October 1939, the US lifted an embargo on selling supplies to warring countries, and were ready to supply Britain and France with weapons, planes, and food. There was a caveat in place though. It stated that American ships were banned from leaving port if they were heading to warring countries including Britain, France, Germany, Ireland, northern Norway, Sweden, Denmark, Holland and the Baltic Sea. This condition was in place because while the law around US neutrality permitted the sale of supplies to belligerents (excluding Germany), the onus was on the warring countries to come and get the supplies from US ports, thus risking their own vessels.

Meanwhile, despite geopolitical tensions rising, soon to be enemies continued to trade with one another, including the raw materials needed for war. In fact, Germany ordered a million tonnes of food from Russia, and considered building an electric railway between the two countries to help transport food. What's more, the Australian Wheat Board put a recommendation up to the federal government to allow wheat to be traded on a barter basis with Japan when it involved certain raw materials that were required by the industrial and manufacturing sectors. In particular, this request included raw materials that were previously sourced from Great Britain.

Australia attempts to avert WWI style wheat headaches

Down in Australia the federal government was seeking advice on how much wheat Britain would require from the upcoming harvest. The UK stated that it would take part of the Australian production, but could not commit to receiving the whole harvest surplus. Their justification included the existence of large world stocks to draw on; the bulkiness of wheat as cargo; the distance to Australia compared to other countries; and the possibility of a depleted shipping fleet in the near future. The British government also agreed that it would buy wheat at the Australian port level, and absorb the risk and cost of moving the grain themselves.

The Australian government expected the British to take only 850,000 tonnes at this point, and only 1.5 million tonnes was needed for domestic Australian use. With that in mind, a surplus of around 2.2 million tonnes of wheat was expected to remain within Australian shores.

To minimise futures surpluses the Australian government began consulting with state leaders about curtailing wheat planting. The plan was to take most of the least productive lands where crops grew at the fringes of viability out of production. This theoretical plan would involve a form of licensing to regulate the wheat sowing area each farmer could do.

The Australian government was also contemplating whether to expand (or more realistically, to restart from an almost non-existent base) the Australian freight ship building industry. The cost of building ships in the UK and delivering the vessels to Australia was already double the pre-war levels.[27] With steel being cheaper in Australia than the UK, it started to make sense to manufacture freight ships locally. However, the urgent need to use all available ship building facilities to fulfill naval orders forced the deferment of the construction of any merchant ships.

WORLD WAR II – THE CURSE OF AUSTRALIA IS PROCRASTINATION

Meanwhile Canada was facing an even bigger challenge. The Canadians had just harvested the second biggest crop on record, and had no agreement at all in place with the British for its export. In fact, the surplus of 11 million tonnes that Canada had at its disposal could supply the UK's annual needs twice over.[28] To compound the challenges the Canadian government faced, all the wheat had been paid for by the Canadian government, and as a result a significant amount of the government's funds were tied up. What's more, the majority of the available storage space was jam-packed, and a huge quantity of stock was being held in transit in railway cars, with some railway companies simply refusing to take any more.

Britain said they would buy 2.7 million tonnes from Canada for a higher price than it could get in other markets (to help relieve congestion), but as a caveat they wanted Canada to close the Winnipeg Grain Exchange. Their argument was that they did not want Canadian grain exporters to be able to sell wheat to the UK at a higher price than neutral countries were able to buy it for from Canada. The Canadian grain trade was not prepared to agree with that requirement, noting that the US was experiencing adverse weather conditions and that prices could rise later in the year. The consequence of that was no large wheat sales were agreed on between the UK and Canada in 1939.

1940 – Food shortages arise despite a global wheat surplus

A dislocation in logistics and trade caused by the war meant that certain regions started to develop food shortages despite there being a global surplus of wheat.

WAR AND WHEAT

The drivers of the shortage included British blockades of continental Europe; German submarine attacks; a lack of insurance for vessels; Germany absorbing continental European supplies from invaded and controlled countries; and insufficient freight to move crops.

A significant amount of US shipping capacity was sitting in ports because its neutrality prevented US ship operators from going to the ports of combatants. Another large proportion of global shipping belonged to other neutral nations. However, many of those vessels were stuck in the ports of combatants while being very slowly searched for contraband before being allowed to move onward.

In early January 1940, the Danube River froze and the volume of supplies moving from Romania to Germany declined substantially. For Germany, the problems caused by the weather were compounded by Russian blockades. Romanian rail traffic was frequently interrupted in Russian occupied rail transit areas. Prior to the war, Germany used to import Balkan wheat through the Black Sea and the Mediterranean to North Sea ports. With Turkey on the allied side this time, that option was also no longer available either. Yugoslavia also suddenly decided to ban the export of food to anyone due to their own shortages.

Once the Danube River thawed and trade started flowing through Russian-occupied Poland, Germany began absorbing so much wheat out of Romania and Bulgaria that the two countries had to begin rationing food supplies.

On the allied side, France started to run out of labour to work in the wheat fields and factories. The shortage resulted in 15,000 men being called

WORLD WAR II – THE CURSE OF AUSTRALIA IS PROCRASTINATION

back from reserves, while females and youths were encouraged to work, with the looming likelihood that it could soon become compulsory. An influx of refugees from adjacent countries that had to be fed and sheltered added to France's challenges. Approximately 3 million refugees had entered France since the start of the war.

To make matters worse, in late January of 1940, the cropping season overseas started to look less optimistic than had been hoped. Due to a particularly dry season in the US, production expectations fell to 20.5 million tonnes compared to 25 million tonnes the year prior. News came out of Argentina that they'd harvested a worse than expected crop of 3.6 million tonnes versus 9 million tonnes the previous year. French and British mobilisation meant that markets were doubtful that a full sowing program had occurred at the end of 1939, and that a successful harvest could be reaped mid-year.

The UK runs short on foreign currency

In early March the UK was running desperately low on US dollars. In order to ration their US dollar reserves, the British government closed off its import market to only include empire countries that accepted Stirling. This way the UK could use currency that it could create itself for buying commodities, and only resort to buying from non-empire countries when all other alternatives were exhausted. In mid-March the British government then moved to nationalise the shipbuilding industry and take control of the entire British merchant service.

WAR AND WHEAT

Germany and Japan ramp up the pressure

In April 1940 Germany invaded Denmark followed by the Netherlands. The Germans quickly moved to take available grain from storage facilities. The grain robbery was made worse by the fact that both countries were far from being self-sufficient. With foreign currency desperately low, Germany demanded Romania pay 30-100% more for German exports while the price it would pay Romania for its goods would remain unchanged. By mid-1940, most of France including its vital heavy industries, mines and wheat growing regions had been lost to the Germans. Reports began to arise about France being on the brink of collapse. In occupied China, the Japanese blockaded French and British occupied concessions.

Meanwhile the British were busy attempting to limit the need for Spain to join the Axis out of necessity. To that end, the British lent money to the Spanish to purchase goods including wheat. That resulted in 100,000 tonnes of wheat being moved from neutral Portugal into Spain to ease their growing shortage of wheat that had resulted from their civil war.

By July, Russia was advancing into Romania and the Germans told the Romanian government to agree to all of Russia's demands for the time being. Reports were frequent of Romanian soldiers clashing with Russian soldiers while pulling back as the Romanian government made area concessions. Russia was busy taking whatever wheat and other goods it could find, including those that had been claimed by Germany earlier. At this stage, Romania had not called up it's 800,000 reservists yet.

WORLD WAR II – THE CURSE OF AUSTRALIA IS PROCRASTINATION

Germany's strategy of rapid expansion runs into roadblocks

Germany's conquests of northern European nations and France were successful when it came to temporarily replenishing their own wheat reserves. However, in the longer term it meant that a considerable proportion of the European population were suddenly reliant on Germany to be fed. If they weren't fed, there would be more civilian unrest and a decline in the ability occupied nations had to produce food themselves. A compounding challenge was that many northern European nations were net grain and fertiliser importers prior to the war. In other words, they were never self-sufficient. As they could no longer import grain or fertiliser because of the British blockade, they had to rely on Germany to supply fertiliser. As a result of the constrained fertiliser availability, northern European agriculture began grinding to a halt.

Australia continues to battle with an oversupply

By August, another Australian harvest was approaching, while stockpiles of wheat from previous harvests were still piled up across the country. While Australia had wheat sales contracts set up with multiple European countries, difficulties in obtaining freight (just like in WWI) were resulting in contracts needing to be cancelled. To remove some of the excess wheat stock, the government started thinking about selling wheat at a discount to local dairy, poultry, and pig farmers in Australia.

WAR AND WHEAT

The UK desperately needed access to pork and dairy product imports due to the loss of northern European markets that were now under Nazi control. What's more, shipping animal protein from Australia amounted to less freight tonnage than shipping the grain to feed animals in the UK. It made sense to start producing and shipping more meat out of Australia rather than just relying on grain exports because it required far less freight capacity. To provide some parameters here, each kilogram of beef in present day 2024 requires roughly 8-12 kilograms of feed, and back in WWII even more grain would have been needed.

Another solution to the local oversupply of wheat was for the government to support the development of a biofuel industry. In the knowledge that their ability to import fuel could soon be constrained, the Australian government had been actively looking into using wheat to create power alcohol (biofuel). In fact, an increasing number of horses were already being utilised in agriculture due to fuel shortages. While the cost of creating a biofuel industry appeared far more expensive than importing diesel, the prospect of soon having fuel shortages was pushing the government towards creating the industry regardless.

Food shortages go from bad to worse in Europe

Dutch poultry production was cut to one third of its pre-war levels due to a shortage of feed, and Norwegian flour millers were being asked to mix wheat with dried grass to make it go further. Northern France was the only remaining notable region in continental Europe that encompassed a large wheat growing area that was

WORLD WAR II – THE CURSE OF AUSTRALIA IS PROCRASTINATION

not fully occupied. That said, it wasn't too far from being fully under Nazi control. Meanwhile, neutral Turkey was the only country in southeast Europe in 1940 with a wheat surplus.

Germany was demanding Yugoslavia deliver 3,500 trucks of wheat immediately to meet their German imposed quota.[29] Yugoslavia needed to deliver 20,000 trucks of wheat and 10,000 of maize in total for the year under their quota. This was a gargantuan task considering their crop was down 30% on the previous year due to floods and a harsh winter. As far as wheat reserves were concerned, Yugoslavia was expected to completely run out by February or March of 1941. For the domestic market in a normal year, 245,000 truckloads of wheat were needed for consumption in Yugoslavia, while in 1939 only 200,000 truckloads worth of wheat were produced.

On August the 26th, Romania finally called up it's 800,000 reservists and banned military leave while the Hungarians, who had constant friction with Romania did the same. The mobilisation concerned Hitler because he was wanting to maintain peace in the Balkans so that it could be used as a bread pantry and an accessible source of oil. Hitler was also hoping that Italy joining the war earlier in the year meant that they could soon invade and defeat Greece. This would clear the road into Turkey and its wheat, and clear the route to the oil reserves of the Middle East. Access to more oil had the potential to prolong the war indefinitely for Germany.

Meanwhile, the Russians were assessing any options to ensure Germany didn't make further inroads into south-eastern Europe. Their aim was to avoid

WAR AND WHEAT

Germany being able to use the region as a springboard to claim Ukraine for its food reserves, and the Russian Caucus region for its oil reserves at all costs. At this point, Russia was already supplying the Greeks with oil and wheat despite being in a non-aggression pact with Germany.

On the 20th of September the Italians attacked Egypt from Italian Libya. Their objective was to access the fertile plains of Alexandria where the vast majority of Egypt's agricultural production came from. They were soon met with British resistance.

In the last days of September, Spain changed their position in the war from being neutral to non-belligerent. Being neutral meant that a country did not support any warring parties, while non-belligerence meant that while the country is not directly involved in the war, it may support one side in ways that do not involve active combat.

Spain's plan was to not impede any stealth operations against British Gibraltar being run by the Axis powers, without actually joining the Axis powers or entering the war. The Spanish were forced to import a large portion of their food after its agricultural capabilities were significantly reduced during its civil war. This meant that if they joined the war on the Axis side, all imports would automatically be blockaded by the British. This was particularly significant because the Germans already had enough on their plate to deal with, let alone feeding the Spanish.

The Japanese had officially joined the Axis powers by September, but stated that the move was only a part of their far east policy. The Japanese stressed that they

WORLD WAR II – THE CURSE OF AUSTRALIA IS PROCRASTINATION

had no intention of fighting Australia, the UK or the US, and were still looking to buy more wheat and wool from Australia.

The bold German dash to South America through North Africa

In early October 1940, Germany enacted a daring plan to create a commodity trade belt from South America, stretching past North Africa, through the strait of Gibraltar, into occupied Axis countries, and on to Germany.

On October the 5th, Germany took control of all of the French colonies in North Africa. The Germans' first objective was to drain north Africa of its wheat reserves. Their strategy involved taking 60% of wheat reserves for themselves, and splitting the remaining 40% between Italy which was an Axis ally, and the new German installed government in Vichy France.[30] Large reserves of phosphate in North Africa were also a prized possession that was destined for Germany to address their agricultural and explosive needs.

As well as stripping North Africa of its food, the Germans were establishing it as a halfway point for trade from South America, particularly Brazil. Germany and Italy were pressing Spain to allow their armies to traverse Spain en mass to take Gibraltar from the British. That way they would be in control of both sides of the entrance to the Mediterranean.

Meanwhile, the Italians and Spaniards were preparing an international zone in Tangiers. Germany had already got the Tangiers media on its side. Influential British citizens like the heads of banks were

WAR AND WHEAT

being arrested with the objective of removing any British trade influence. Lufthansa airline pilots and ground crews had already landed in Dakar on the west coast of north Africa, and German agents were negotiating with South American shippers to open a service to Dakar.

Allies begin pre-emptive measures against Japan

In mid-October, the US removed wheat subsidies for shipments going to China because of concerns Japan was getting access to the wheat enroute. Further to that, the UK and US started preparing plans for a Japanese economic and military blockage. One of the main objectives was to restrict oil flows to the Japanese to limit their ability to take the conflict further south towards Australia. At the time, Japan was reportedly processing the oil it had previously imported from Texas into aviation fuel.

The government assesses whether it should tell farmers how much land to farm

With national wheat stocks still large and the export channels clogged by freight challenges, the Australian government was closely looking at possibly implementing planting area restrictions for the early 1941 planting season. Coincidentally, drought started to creep into New South Wales and Victoria. In early September 1940, the Federal government sent a wheat market stabilisation plan to state governments for consideration.

In order to balance supply and demand, the plan involved growers receiving licenses limiting how many

WORLD WAR II – THE CURSE OF AUSTRALIA IS PROCRASTINATION

hectares they could plant with grain. It also included a requirement for them to cut their wheat crop for hay (as opposed to allowing it to turn to grain) when it was requested by the government. The government also made the caveat that the program would only apply for national production under 3.8 million tonnes, from which point it could not guarantee its minimum price of 3s 6d per bushel.

The main purpose of the wheat stabilisation scheme would be to reduce production and ensure reasonable prices to small farmers with less than 2,000 acres, who constituted approximately 80% of the nation's growers. The most important thing was to keep the majority of the sector running – even if was in a lower gear.

By early November, progress for expanding the nations logistics system, to move more wheat from rural areas to port, had been put on hold due to a lack of materials and machinery for its construction.

Germany makes a move into Romania

German military forces occupied Romania with limited casualties in early November. While Germany didn't want Romania to become involved in the war, it was concerned that Russia would soon occupy the majority of the country for its own needs. Not surprisingly, tensions were rising exponentially on the borders between the German and Soviet occupied countries. Furthermore, farmers in the occupied countries were refusing to farm their land, thereby limiting the future supplies of food that would be available to Germany.

Germany continued to pile pressure on Yugoslavia to accept the 'new European order', and to join Hungary,

WAR AND WHEAT

Slovakia and Romania as an associate of the Axis power. The Yugoslavians previously had a negative relationship with Italy, and hence they were less than enthusiastic about joining the axis, though they only had a limited army to resist. Meanwhile Russia was actively discouraging Bulgaria from joining the Axis group as the relationship between Germany and Russia continued to worsen.

Tensions between Russia and Germany close to boiling point as 1941 begins

In early 1941, Germany was optimistically hoping Russia would fold and supply them with the resources they needed for the war. Germany's aim was to establish a situation where Russia was to Germany, what the US was to Britain: an endless arsenal of food, oil and metals.

That situation became less likely as tensions between Russia and Germany came close to boiling point. Newspapers at the time were predicting a peaceful German invasion of Bulgaria, with no Soviet intervention. At the same time, Soviet ministers were suddenly being called back to Moscow from Yugoslavia, Hungary, Romania and Bulgaria.

Communists across Bulgaria began sending around leaflets claiming that the soviets wouldn't let German soldiers into Bulgaria. In Romania, communists began sabotaging railway lines, while the government cut off cross border telephone communications both in and out of Romania as talks of a Romanian civil war began circulating. The export of wheat, oats and oil from Romania was suddenly prohibited, including to Germany. In early March, German troops moved into

WORLD WAR II – THE CURSE OF AUSTRALIA IS PROCRASTINATION

Bulgaria without bloodshed, and Russia complained that the Bulgarians were submitting to the aggression of the Germans without a fight.

US steps up support at the hindrance of Australia

British dominions including Australia were worried about the UK getting involved in the US lend-lease agreement because it could then receive unlimited foodstuffs from the US, and not pay a penny while the war lasted. All payments would come under a loan to the US. It was an odd decision considering the UK could 'print' more British pounds and use them to pay for Australian wheat with ease.

Around the same time, the Australian commodities sector started pondering what a post war trade environment with the UK would look like. The UK's economy would no longer be large enough to be able to absorb all of the commodities of the dominions. To ensure Australian industries would not shrink in a post war environment, many international trade barriers would need to be broken down to be able to trade freely outside of the imperial system.

Germany makes final preparations to invade Russia

In early June 1941, German agents across neutral capitals were circulating messages that Hitler was planning to attack Russia very soon. Germany was disappointed by the lack of economic help they had received from Russia since the start of the war, and started to amass troops on the Russian border.

WAR AND WHEAT

Within communist circles, there was significant division about the Soviet Union's relationship with Nazi Germany. Reportedly, the head of Comintern (which was an international organisation overseen by the Communist Party in the Soviet Union), M Dimitrov, was advocating for Russia to declare war with Hitler before Germany became unbeatable. However, the vice-secretary of the communist party, Zhdanov, wanted to establish a full military alliance with Hitler in exchange for the right for Russia to expand towards India.

By mid-June, Stalin was aware that German preparations for a possible attack on Russia were virtually complete. There was a line of military divisions reaching all the way from German occupied Norway to Ukraine. Russia wasn't caught off guard, they had already put a strong concentration of troops in Ukraine to protect the breadbasket and access to the oil rich Caucuses.

The commentators of the day were writing that Germany didn't do this to invade Russia, but to pressure Russia into providing Germany with the war supplies they needed. In exchange for this, Germany would offer a free hand to Stalin in relation to Russia's advances into Asia, including India and Japan.

By the 16th of June, 120 German military divisions and 140 Russian divisions had accumulated on the border separating Russia and Germany. By this time, Germany was running out of options, and it could see that their food reserves would soon start to run low. Germany was actively trying to threaten Russia into signing an agreement where they would get access to almost unlimited credit to purchase Russian cereals, oil and other raw materials. Earlier in the war Russian deliveries were made only in return for liquid foreign

WORLD WAR II – THE CURSE OF AUSTRALIA IS PROCRASTINATION

currency or manufactured goods. With the Germans running low on foreign currency reserves, as well as on manufactured goods due to shortages of raw materials and labour, they could no longer foot the bill in the same way. As a result, Russia's supply of goods to Germany started to dry up. Stalin was trying to avoid the war until he had built up a structure of security that was unchallengeable, but as history can attest, this goal was never reached.

On the 22nd of June 1941, Germany invaded Russia just as the Russian grain harvest was kicking off. The Germans hoped to take Ukraine quickly and move through to the Caucuses to access Russia's oil. At that time, Russia produced on average around 25 million tonnes of wheat, with 6 million tonnes coming from Ukraine.[31]

Interestingly, western views on Russia changed very quickly once Germany invaded it. Overnight, Russia went from being a threat to be feared, to a friend that must be fought beside and aided. The tone was captured by an article published in Australia in June 1941. "There is no time to quibble over whether Stalin is redder than Hitler or the OGPU worse than the Gestapo. We must fight with Russia, fight as never before. Hitler and Germany are our enemies. We cannot mix with bogy-bogy stories that Russia may have deserted the democracies in their hour of need. She may yet be our salvation." This was written by Stewart Campbell and published in the *Sunday Pictorial*.

Three days after Germany's invasion, the US agreed to supply Russia with everything it required. They also lifted restrictions on Russian money and assets in the US which had been frozen since they defaulted on foreign loans during the 1917 revolution.

WAR AND WHEAT

Global wheat producers try to solve the wheat glut

The international wheat conference met in July, with American republics and British Commonwealth nations present. The meeting was focussed on figuring out how to make sure wheat industries in allied exporting countries were not bankrupted by the large global wheat surplus. The strategies they were considering included compulsory acreage reductions in participating countries.

Acreage restrictions worked well in theory, but in reality, there was no guarantee that everyone would abide by the restrictions. More importantly, there was a practical problem that Australia was soon to experience. The problem came out of the circumstances of acreage restrictions being implemented in the same year as a drought. Under those circumstances, it wouldn't only be a case of low yields, but the artificially diminished area for planting could lead to a sudden regional or global shortage.

The big risk was if this occurred just as the allies start winning the war and require extra food to feed starving liberated populations. This would not only be catastrophic from a humanitarian perspective, but also from a geopolitical strategic perspective. Food shortages could result in civil unrest, revolutions, and foreign interference in liberated nations.

Trade noose tightened over Japan but with strange caveats

On the 30th of July 1941, almost a complete cessation of trade by Britain and the US with Japan was complete. There was an immediate freezing of Japanese assets in

WORLD WAR II – THE CURSE OF AUSTRALIA IS PROCRASTINATION

the UK. However, trade by strict licencing overseen by the US government was allowed. The British and the US were reportedly reluctant to enact a full ban or blockade because of the impact it would have on British dominions that exported to Japan, and were already heavily impacted by the war.

Diesel shortage prompts Australian government to accelerate the development of a biofuel industry

Support for a biofuel industry in Western Australia was growing. It was being accelerated by a diesel shortage and a growing oversupply of grain on the domestic market. The government began investigating the viability of this approach by experimenting with wheat distillation. Distillation could cost 4 shillings per gallon, and one bushel of wheat would yield two gallons of power alcohol. The proposed plan was for a plant with the capacity to use 20 thousand tonnes a year of wheat to be set up at an estimated cost of 70,000 pounds.

US spearheads a plan to develop a post-war relief plan for agriculture export nations

As the war progressed the national wheat agreement conference was moved from London to Washington, symbolising the shifting global power centre. The draft agreement that came out of the conference stated that a treaty would set up a government-controlled world granary. The intention was to eventually provide large wheat volumes for post-war relief in Europe. It was agreed that the strategy would also need to deal with the current global oversupply. If the oversupply was not dealt with, farmers would not find it economically viable to keep farming and production would decline. The decline in production could coincide with the end of the war when there would be a sudden surge in demand. To keep farmers operating, higher global prices were needed for the time being.

The draft plan involved putting export quotas and acreage controls in place for the world's largest exporters who were not directly impacted by war at the time. The countries in question were Australia, Argentina, Canada, and the US.

On the 27th of August, the US government approved a significant amount of spending for the military, but it had not yet confirmed whether the US would join the war effort directly. Meanwhile, British and Russian forces invaded pro-German Iran to secure oil reserves and create a route for western supplies to be brought into Russia through the Persian Gulf.

Italy can no longer supply Germany with wheat

By late September 1941, food shortages in Italy led to rioting across Milan and Turin following news that bread rationing was planned to take effect soon. The wheat content of bread had already been reduced by 25% since the start of the war, with corn and potatoes replacing wheat.

Mussolini stated that the wheat crop was 7.15 million tonnes, which was marginally up on the year prior. Even though it was an increase on the previous year, it was still insufficient to cover the needs of the Italian population and occupied territories. For Germany, the shortage meant that Italy was not able to supply it with the wheat it had promised it an Axis member.

WORLD WAR II – THE CURSE OF AUSTRALIA IS PROCRASTINATION

With Italy unable to supply Germany with wheat, there was even more incentive for Germany to break through Russian lines and access its wheat supplies. By October, the Nazi's were making their way towards Moscow and into Eastern Ukraine, with the aim of making it to the oil rich regions. Grozny, an oil rich region in the Caucuses, was producing 12% of all Russian oil at the time and housed large refineries.[32] The region also housed the Rostselmash agricultural machinery factory employing 20,000 workers. By capturing the plant, not only could Germany take the current Russian grain reserves, but it could also infringe on Russia's ability to produce more in future years, limiting its ability to fight back.

Britain officially runs out of space for wheat

By November, British wheat reserves within and outside of the UK were so large that it started sending its Canadian stockpiles to Russia. An excessively oversupplied Britain became a significant concern to an overseas wheat exporter and supplier like Australia. Concern over lack of future UK demand added even more incentive to build a domestic grain-based fuel industry.

Pearl Harbour brings America into the war

1941 finished with Japan attacking Pearl Harbour on the 7th of December, bringing America directly into WWII. Apart from the obvious challenges to Australia of having a new foe to deal with, the Japanese had purchased a cargo of Australian wheat just before the outbreak of hostilities and had not paid 350,000 pounds owed for it. To the relief of the Australian wheat board, the UK took the funds out of frozen Japanese assets in London.

Meanwhile, the Australian government continued negotiations over the international wheat agreement to address the global wheat oversupply. With the time for the planting of next year's crop fast approaching, Australian growers were demanding the government provide them clarity on how much they should plant. The government initially stated there would be no reduction in the cropping area at the beginning of 1942. However, by the end of the month, the government did a backflip and stated that there would be a definite acreage restriction placed on all growers cropping more than 300 acres. The government wanted just enough land being cropped that it required only one man per farm to do the job.

The government failed to factor in that a reduction in the planted area was already likely to be underway across the east coast. Conditions were already drier heading into the planting period compared to last year while fertiliser and labour shortages were becoming concerning.

1942 – Allies bolster the Russian front

Supplies continued to pour into Russia through Iran from the US and UK to bolster it against Germany. Everything from military supplies, to wheat, to wool, to wolfram and copper was being sent, with the UK organising the logistics. The goods came into the Persian Gulf and moved up to northern Iran where Russian soldiers would take it further.

WORLD WAR II – THE CURSE OF AUSTRALIA IS PROCRASTINATION

In June, Italy requested Germany hand over Tunisia because it had large reserves of phosphates and large cropping acreage in coastal areas. Meanwhile in Vichy France riots broke out after a list was released to the public stating who would be sent to Germany as labour.

Back in Australia, the cost involved in farming continued to escalate with the Australian government increasing the cost of fertiliser. The principal reason for the increase was the freight rate charged on goods imported into Australia.

International wheat agreement details come out

In July 1942, details of the finalised International Wheat Agreement that became active on the 27th of June were released to the public.[33] What it boiled down to was that there would be production limits imposed on four key exporting countries and the UK. They were Argentina, Australia, Canada, and the US. Further to that, there was to be the immediate establishment of an intergovernmental wheat relief pool for war-stricken countries to access reserves. Contributions of 2.7 million tonnes were required from participants, with subsequent amounts being requested as and when needed.

The Australian government finally gives the green light for the creation of a biofuel industry

In November 1942, the Australian government decided to construct four distillery plants to go into crop producing areas. The aim was for farmers to be able to supply their crops to a local facility to turn it into biofuel. The by-product of that process could then be fed to cattle to offset the higher cost of biofuel production versus petrol.

Essentially, biofuel plants would be converting the starch content of wheat into sugar which would become pure alcohol for fuel. The plan was for the Cowra plant on the east coast of Australia to be doing this at the rate of three million gallons a year, with the plan for three more plants of similar capacity to be in operation by 1944.

The first nail in the coffin for Nazi expansion

In late November, the allies took back French Africa. That move destroyed Germany's plans to create a supply chain taking raw goods from south America into the European Axis territory. At the same time, the action cut off Italy from much needed food and fertiliser reserves.

1943 – Push back against the Germans

1943 started with the Russians pushing back against the Germans in the Caucuses with the help of western supplies. Turkey remained out of the war but had 1 million troops at the ready, and was actively supplying the allies critical materials in exchange for food. The UN was sending Turkey wheat in return for chromium being sent to the US, the UK and the USSR.

This wasn't only about addressing their own needs, but also making sure that the chromium didn't wind up in the hands of the Nazi's. The value of Chromium was that it has wide variety of applications, from armour plating to weapons manufacturing.

WORLD WAR II – THE CURSE OF AUSTRALIA IS PROCRASTINATION

Solutions to labour shortages

Labour shortages due to the war led to countries implementing a variety of solutions. In the UK, labour shortages led to an uptake in farm machinery, with the number of tractors across the country increasing from just 50,000 in 1939, to 90,000 by 1942.[34] Australia employed prisoners of war because it didn't have the infrastructure available to construct tractors, and it only had a very limited ability to import tractors due to freight challenges.

By the second half of 1943, the number of men engaged in rural industries throughout Australia decreased from roughly 500,000 prior to the war, to a mere 131,000.[35] On April 5th in 1943, the Australian government approved the employment of up to 1,000 Italian Prisoners of War to work in rural industries without guards being required. The hygiene and health of the workers were to be taken care of by their employers. Then on May 14, the war cabinet upped the ante and approved a recommendation that 10,000 Italian prisoners of war should be put to work to help meet Australia's requirement to provide bulk foodstuff to its allies under an international agreement.

The price of POW labour was only 1/7th of a typical Australian wage. Needless to say, this situation concerned local unions who demanded an edict by which no employer could refuse a job to an Australian seeking employment over a POW. One year later, 12,000 POWs were working in the agricultural space, with 1,839 assisting with cropping in particular.

The employment of cheaper labour supported farmers who were dealing with squeezed profit margins due to frozen commodity prices and rising costs in the form of labour and fertiliser. Later in the year, Australia started importing farm machinery under the US lend-lease agreement.

Don't minimise, maximise!

By the middle of 1943, the Australian government's attitude started to shift from needing to minimise the amount of wheat produced, to recognising that the world was likely to need a significant volume of Australian wheat in the not-too-distant future. At the same time, Victoria which is positioned at the bottom of the east coast of Australia, started to enter a severe drought.

By early August, despite the international wheat agreement being officially finalised, it was discovered that the US and Argentina had started increasing their total wheat area instead of reducing it. The Australian Wheat Board took this as a sign that they wanted to snatch away Australian export market share.

With that threat on the horizon, the Australian Wheat Board started inquiring with the government if it would be possible to place wheat stocks in the Middle East so that market share could instantly be increased once countries bordering the Mediterranean were reconquered by allied troops.

Only three weeks later, the UK ordered a substantial amount of Australian flour. This was significant because ordering flour assumes that it would soon be used, otherwise it goes off much quicker than unprocessed wheat grain. The British ordered flour for various destinations, including the Middle East.

WORLD WAR II – THE CURSE OF AUSTRALIA IS PROCRASTINATION

It was likely that this was an early sign that the UK believed the war had started to turn in the allies' favour, and large volumes of flour would soon be needed to feed freed populations. The Australian Controller of Food asked that manpower be made available to enable the mills to operate with a three-shift capacity.

September 1943 ushers in an acceleration of Axis losses

By the end of September 1943, Fascist Italy had collapsed, and Russia claimed a string of victories on the eastern front. Hungary was growing concerned about what would happen next, with German troops occupied elsewhere and unable to protect it from Russian troops coming from the east.

In late September, Canada's minister of trade announced the suspension of trading on the Winnipeg Grain Exchange, and stated that the government run Canadian Wheat Board would take over from the following Monday's close. Under the new arrangement, the Canadian government would provide wheat at subsidised prices for domestic purchasers like flour millers out of government owned reserves. This was done to ensure that farmers could keep receiving a viable price so that they did not reduce area planted or production. With the war heading in the allies favour, large volumes were suddenly what was needed.

In November 1943, Australia sent 50,000 tonnes of wheat to India.[36] The country was in incredibly poor shape, with Bengal in a state of famine. The main challenge was that Australia had the grain India needed, but it continued to struggle on acquiring freight.

WAR AND WHEAT

Post-war relief efforts are quantified

On the 11th of the 11th in 1943, the 44 united and associated nations signed an agreement to create a UN relief and rehabilitation administration.[37] Contributions would need to be made by all signatories, with the initial idea of having 1% of each nations GDP committed.

The aim of these contributions was to help provide the minimum necessary needs for war ravaged countries to carry out their own rehabilitation. Preliminary estimates of the requirements for the countries in Europe came in at 46 million tonnes of materials. This included medical supplies, food, clothing, seed, and machinery for the following six months. Half of this was expected to be found in Europe itself. The requirement in relation to vessels needed to import goods was estimated at 1,500 ships with a total freight capacity of 10,000 tonnes each.

It was also estimated that Britain's share of the relief provisions would be as high as 9.5 million tonnes, with 1.5 million tonnes coming from Australia. There were concerns that Germany would burn everything in its path including food as they retreated. Of course, if that was the case it would increase the total relief requirement. Estimates were that 19 European countries with a combined population of 188 million people would be in dire need of help. In addition to that there were 41.5 million Italians and 72 million Germans to take into account. This amounted to a grand total of 301.5 million people requiring assistance.

WORLD WAR II – THE CURSE OF AUSTRALIA IS PROCRASTINATION

The Australian government turns on the agricultural production taps

December 1943 was a turning point. The Australian government planned to increase production in line with its commitments to the UN for post-war relief. W. A Scully, the Minster of Commerce and Agriculture, announced new commonwealth plans for stepping up production within all major Australian food industries. The Minister stated that Australia's part in the global allied strategy included being a food depot for the United Nations (UN). Food heading to Russia would also need to be continued even after the collapse of the axis. Additionally, neither Britian nor Ireland were self-sufficient in food, while Spain and Portugal were both on restricted diets.

Cheap feed wheat began being released to the market by the Australian government so that more dairy, pork, and poultry could be produced. At the same time, meat consumption in Australia needed to be reduced by 20% so that overseas demand could be met. The Australian government had promised that 15,000 men would be secured from conscription to work in the rural industries three months earlier, but only 4,000 had been released at that point.

1944 – Victory over Axis powers edges closer

By April 1944 the Germans had been pushed back by the Russians to their critical Ploesti oil fields in Romania. The British, becoming more confident about the war ending in their favour, started providing citizens with an almost pure wheat loaf.

WAR AND WHEAT

At the time, American government officials played down speculation of Germany running out of food. However, commentators were writing that the German retreat from Russia would have far-reaching consequences for its ability to feed itself. The previous summer, 4,000 food trains crossed the soviet frontier, taking half a million tons of wheat, butter, eggs, poultry, pork, and vegetable oils to Germany.

In Greece, two warring guerrilla parties met in Cairo to settle their differences in order to fight the common foe – Germany. They asked for the allied mission to supply them with food and other aid according to their share in operations against Germany. The British Ministry of Economic Warfare announced that it had already been sending 20,000 tons of foodstuff to Greece every month, and in total had already sent 150,000 tonnes of wheat their way.

Keeping consumer prices low is more important than higher profit margins for farmers

Australia had accumulated 4.3 million tonnes of wheat in storage by mid-1944. That was 50% more than the amount that was held one year earlier, and an overbearing amount compared to the normal peace-time carry over of around 0.4 million tonnes. Freight to the UK, which was only occasionally available, cost four times more than it did at the beginning of the war.

To increase the production of dairy and meat in line with the UN directed post-war plan, the Australian government asked the Australian Wheat Board to sell wheat at a cheaper rate to local stock feeders than what it was receiving through the exported price at the

WORLD WAR II – THE CURSE OF AUSTRALIA IS PROCRASTINATION

time. In response, the AWB reminded the government that it would need to subsidise the gap in order to maintain stability in payments to farmers. If they didn't, the potential was there for farmers to see it as less worthwhile to plant out as much land as they could.

Later in the year, the government would go on to defend its strategy. The government stated that it had been willing to sell wheat locally for a cheaper price than it exported it for because it had committed to keeping consumer food prices low during the war, especially in light of prices elsewhere skyrocketing. The future Prime Minister Menzies said that "the policy of keeping costs down outweighed any benefit which could possibly be secured by chasing overseas prices up to [overseas] inflation."[38]

On the 2nd of May 1944, it was also revealed that a government censorship department had been censoring the level of dissatisfaction being expressed by farmers about the minimum wheat price that appeared in the media. Interestingly, censorship of the media was allowed when the censorship department believed the criticism would prejudice the outcome of the war against the government.

What happens to dominion exports after the war?

With the war moving strongly in favour of the West, more of the domestic Australian focus started to turn towards where exports of dominions (specifically Australia and Canada) could find new markets in a post-war world. While the UK would continue to exist as a market, at this point it was heavily indebted, and the question arose around how it could pay a competitive price compared to other buyers.

WAR AND WHEAT

During the depression years following WWI, the British economy suffered greatly. The consequence was an inability to purchase large enough quantities of wheat from dominions. The fear was that the same situation would occur following WWII. The concept of having a self-contained and self-sufficient British empire trading system, separate from the rest of the world, no longer held up. The next Imperial conference moved to assessing how the commonwealth nations could integrate into a global system. As context, Imperial conferences were gatherings of government leaders from self-governing colonies and dominions of the British Empire.

Even while the war was ongoing, it made little economic sense for Australia to sell wheat to Britain. Canada had a mutual aid agreement with Britain where it would sell wheat to it on more favourable pricing terms than Australia could. That meant that in order for Australia to get any exports to Britain, it would have to sell them at a similar price. It soon made more sense for Australia, especially since British storage was full, to export to non-traditional markets like US, Mexico, Peru, Ecuador, Fiji and South Africa.

Canada suddenly goes from an excess wheat surplus to a possible shortage

Canada's supplies started to rapidly decrease following increased exports and domestic use, as well as the impact of prior production restrictions. At the time, Canada was exporting large volumes of wheat to surrendered Italy, partially freed Greece, and Russia.

WORLD WAR II – THE CURSE OF AUSTRALIA IS PROCRASTINATION

And just like Australia, they were also increasing livestock feed consumption in order to meet the UN's post-war relief program.

Reduced supplies being available throughout the grain supply chain forced the government to reverse a law it had in place limiting the sale of wheat by farmers. Market commentators were estimating Canadian ending wheat stocks by July 31, 1944 would be 40% lower than the year prior.

Meanwhile the United States Department of Agriculture (USDA) was expecting a record US wheat crop of just over 27 million tonnes following a very wet spring.[39] The US had also significantly ramped up livestock feeding and biofuel production to deal with the earlier surplus. In fact, it was ramped up to such an extent that supply and demand were thrown out of kilter, and supply soon started to disappear in the same way that Canada had experienced.

While the USDA wouldn't state that the reduced availability was alarming, grain merchants started urging the government to curtail the use of wheat for feed. The risk was having a smaller crop the following year due to drought, but still having the new strong domestic demand that had been built up during the war.

Western help being provided to the Soviet Union had continued throughout this period, and no doubt drew down on allied wheat stocks. From October 1941 (3 months after Germany's invasion of Russia) to the end of April 1944, the US sent 8 million tonnes of war supplies in the form of equipment and food to Russia. This included 8,872 aircraft, 3,724 tanks and nearly 207,000 vehicles. Great Britain also sent over one million tonnes which included 3,384 aircraft and 4,292 tanks, while Canada sent 450,000 tonnes, including 20,000 tons of wheat and flour and 1,188 tanks.

International Wheat Agreement Committee tries to fix global pricing

Throughout June 1944, there was a significant amount of discussion taking place around the International Wheat Agreement with the idea of possibly trying to fix the global wheat price before the end of the war. An earlier conference had tried to fix the global oversupply by implementing wheat planting limitations, but they hadn't tried setting export pricing. Furthermore, the wheat planting constraints failed to deal with the global oversupply and resultant low prices.

Australia, just like Canada, was heading into a wheat shortage but more severe

Dry conditions on the east coast of Australia were worsening by August 1944. It was feared that the drought would compound the production downgrade being experienced as a result of the artificially reduced area that was planted earlier in the year. The scenario of a deficit of wheat in NSW began to look like a possibility. There were concerns over how NSW supplies could be replenished given the long-distance domestic transport challenges that were being experienced at the time. The challenges included truck and fuel limitations being prevalent across the country; different railway gauges limiting railway transport between states; and a lack of ships limiting sea freight moving between the states.

WORLD WAR II – THE CURSE OF AUSTRALIA IS PROCRASTINATION

The federal government came out with an announcement about more fertiliser being made available for farmers to boost their crop yields. The shortage of fertiliser in Australia had resulted from Japan's occupation of Nauru in August 1942. In 1943 the imports of superphosphate coming into Australia were a mere 500,000 tonnes.[40] This was half of the pre-war total. Typically, Australia required 1 million tonnes, 400,000 tonnes of which would be used in the production of wheat, cereals and hay. In the 1944 farming season, the availability of fertiliser fell to 114,000 tonnes. With Australia willing to support the US's post-war European aid plan, but unable to boost production due in part to superphosphate shortages, the United Nations and Imperial Fertiliser Committee came to the rescue and made additional fertiliser shipments available to assist the Australian production program.

By early October, the possibility of a food shortage in Australia started becoming more realistic, with national wheat production expected to fall to 1.4 million tonnes. This was the third smallest production figure recorded since the start of the century. The situation was tragic. Not just because of its severity and impact on Australian farmers. It was also tragic because it came at the same time as Australia's agricultural resources were most desperately needed for the enormous post-war relief effort in Europe.

International wheat agreement – new agreement reached

The Australian Secretary for Agriculture reported that a new phase in the International Wheat Agreement had been reached in October 1944. The export market was set to be divided between the four largest (and currently capable) wheat producing countries of the world. They were the United States, Australia, Canada and Argentina. There would be 12.2 million tonnes of wheat in total that could be exported between these nations annually.

The US received 16% of the allotment. This was a small proportion due to the increased domestic demand for wheat in the US which was developed during the war. Canada would receive 42%, and an undisclosed division would occur in relation to the remaining 44% that was being shared between Australia and Argentina.

Throughout WWII, in an attempt to support farmers, there had been multiple attempts to implement minimum or maximum prices, export quotas, and planting restrictions. In the end, due to the large producers like the USSR and Argentina refusing to participate, the agreements had limited impact on the world market.

More European territory liberated from the Nazis

In early November 1944, Greece was entirely free from the Germans and their demand for aid started to accelerate. At the time, Greece was needing 60,000 tonnes of aid a month. The aid was initially supplied by British and American military stocks that had been accumulated in the Middle East.

Meanwhile, the Netherlands was partly liberated by November, but continued to suffer significant food shortages. The Dutch government had 200,000 tonnes of wheat stocks stored in the US, but due to the priority of military operations, it was unable to obtain the required shipping space. There was

WORLD WAR II – THE CURSE OF AUSTRALIA IS PROCRASTINATION

no prospect of immediate relief for agricultural production because much of the soil had been deliberately flooded by the retreating Nazi's opening of the sluice gates. The sluice gates had been Hollands protection against the sea for centuries.

1945 – The last year of the war

The wheat shortage in Australia continued to grow. In January, the operations of flour mills were restricted to two shifts a day rather than the usual three. The initial objective to use grain to produce as much dairy and meat as possible for the UN's post-war recovery effort was the put-on hold. The local shortage became so bad that the grain that had been allocated for the feed sector had to be reduced.

By March the estimate of the harvest size was coming in even smaller than first expected and calculations were being made on how much it would cost to import wheat from overseas. The government would need to compete with countries currently at war. When including the cost of transport and insurance, the cost was multiple times more than the price the government paid local farmers for their wheat.

By April, global food supply issues were starting to pop-up as quickly as peace approached. Drought in Australia and other countries had reduced production. Flood and frost in Britain reduced their most recent harvest, and even potatoes started to be in short supply for the first time during the war.

Shipping was also difficult because the requirements in Europe coincided with a peak demand in the pacific where fighting with the Japanese was still underway.

WAR AND WHEAT

By May, with two months left before harvest time, European production was estimated to drop by 5-10% compared to the year prior.

War in Europe ends

On the 8th of May, Nazi Germany capitulated to the allies and the race to feed the freed starving millions began. With Germany entirely occupied by the Allies, the task of feeding an entire nation needed to be dealt with. There was consensus that a famine over winter was very likely, at least in most of the British zone. German soil was generally poor following back-to-back seasons of intense farming. 4 million tonnes of food had been imported from the Ruhr region before the war, but it was now occupied by the Soviets. Prior to the war 1.5 million tonnes of food was being imported from bordering nations, something that would be impossible now.

By August, the wheels of German industries started turning again. This meant that the chemicals and fertiliser needed for agriculture were once again in production. Britain and America were proceeding with large grain shipments as well.

In Australia, the shortage of wheat became so acute that while Europe was starving, the US would go onto divert a 100,000 tonnes shipment of wheat to Australia. While there was still surplus wheat left over in Western Australia, a combination of factors including union strikes, rain and domestic shipping difficulties made it all but impossible to move it to the east coast throughout 1945. The government would go on to

WORLD WAR II – THE CURSE OF AUSTRALIA IS PROCRASTINATION

boost the minimum price paid to farmers and scrap any acreage limitation policies for the future.

Meanwhile, on the 23rd of August the US ended the Lend-Lease program which financed, fed, and armed the western world and Russia in the fight against Nazi Germany and Japan. Nine days later on September 2nd Japan laid down arms and surrendered after the American air force dropped atomic bombs on Hiroshima and Nagasaki. The United States Department of Agriculture estimated that the world faced more hunger in the first 12 months of peace than during the last years of war.[41]

WAR AND WHEAT

CHAPTER THREE

From COVID to Ukraine – A New Global Conflict is Brewing

Global wheat prices were in the doldrums in late 2019. While grain stocks were low, so was the demand for grain. A year prior, a deadly disease had swept through the world's largest hog herd. It is estimated that in 2018 nearly half of China's 450 million hogs ended up either dying from African Swine Fever or being culled to stop the spread.[46] As the number of hogs declined, so did the demand for grain to feed them, and the volume of Chinese imports. At the time, China had already become the world's largest soybean importer, and it was on the way to becoming the world's largest corn and wheat importer as well. That's what made the impact of reduced Chinese demand so severe. For context, during the year prior to African Swine Fever, China imported a mind boggling 94 million tonnes of soy alone.

On the political front, former US President Donald Trump was busy exchanging tariff shots with China. China's temporary levying of tariffs on US soybeans was the most famous case of trade barriers in agriculture markets so far. China's retaliatory tariff was meant to send a message to the world's largest economy that China had the fire power to hit back. While it did

FROM COVID TO UKRAINE – A NEW GLOBAL CONFLICT IS BREWING

send a message initially, the impact was short-lived because China had no choice but to return to buying US soybeans in 2020. Globally there are only two large exporters of soybeans, the US and Brazil. The US-China trade war marked the beginning of a rapid rise in government involvement in global commodity markets.

By the end of 2019, Chicago Board of Trade (CBOT) Wheat futures slowly crept 8% higher compared to the beginning of the year, finishing at 560 US cents per bushel.[42] Many market commentators considered the low prices to be reflective of a market that was too complacent considering how low global wheat stocks were.

Australia was living in a world of its own

Meanwhile, Australia was enveloped in one of the worst droughts on record. Wheat production had rapidly declined, wheat stocks in storage were disappearing, and the grains industry was close to running on fumes. There was almost nothing left. National wheat production declined from a record 32 million tonnes in 2016, to 21 million tonnes in 2017, just under 18 million tonnes in 2018, and it bottomed out at 14.5 million tonnes in 2019. That was the lowest amount produced in over a decade.[43]

The East Coast was by far the most heavily impacted region during the first two years of the drought. Prices reached record levels. In fact, the price difference between the west and east coast became so large that grain was even being shipped from Western Australian ports to the east coast. This was a rarity. Prices got so high for feed grains that odd commodities

WAR AND WHEAT

like almond hulls started making their way into the livestock feed rations. There were even reports of batches of Tim-Tam biscuits that weren't fit for human consumption being fed to pigs.

By 2019, the severity and longevity of the drought in Western Australia resulted in exports to the east coast drying up completely. Conditions became so bad that in the middle of May, the government even gave permission for a bulk vessel of high protein Canadian wheat to be shipped into Australia for the milling sector to use.

The desperate act of bringing wheat into Australia was like a line in the sand. It showed that it made more economic sense to import wheat from Canada than trying to coax it out of the hands of the few remaining farmers that still had the wheat on hand, waiting for prices to go up.

The prolonged drought dragged a whole group of small and mid-tier grain traders into bankruptcy, and caused severe hardship for farmers. Farmers who had contracted grain sales at the start of the season had nothing to deliver at harvest time, and were significantly out of pocket. Water shortages became so severe that by the end of 2019, many towns across Australia were coming close to the point of needing water to be trucked in for human consumption because many of the local rivers had dried up entirely.

To make matters worse, the east coast of Australia experienced some of the worst bush fires in the country's history leading into Christmas. The fires resulted in large tracts of farmland being torched and Sydney being blanketed in a shroud of thick grey smoke for the last weeks of 2019. Compounding the impact of severe

FROM COVID TO UKRAINE – A NEW GLOBAL CONFLICT IS BREWING

drought and plumes of smoke, news of a new highly transmissible and deadly disease in Wuhan China started making its way into Australian media.

Australian farmers breathe a sigh of relief

In January 2020, the entire Australian agricultural industry, from farmers to rural bankers, breathed a sigh of relief. The three-year drought that tormented rural Australia had finally broken. Rainfall had suddenly covered both the west and east coasts. However, as the harvest wasn't due until late October, local prices continued to trade at record levels.

In the initial weeks of 2020, Covid was slow to be taken seriously. This soon to be once-in-a-century global derailment felt like a non-event for Australia, a country isolated by vast distances and oceans.

It wasn't until the 25th of January that the first case of Covid was detected on Australian soil. At this point the main concern of the Australian agricultural sector was the 'cost' of Covid shutting down the Chinese economy and the resulting decline of import demand. At the time, roughly 30% of Australia's agricultural produce was exported to China.

In China, the first three months of the pandemic were marked by nationwide shutdowns, including at ports. By late February, the initial shutdown period was over, and the movement of goods into China was able to slowly resume. Vessels began being offloaded, and truck workers gradually came back to work to move grain from ports to their destination. To avoid further outbreaks, port employees were reportedly paid multiples of normal wage rates to live and work on-site for months.

WAR AND WHEAT

In the middle of March, as cases continued to rocket higher globally, and amid a significant amount of pushback from China, the World Health Organisation declared Covid-19 to be a global Pandemic. The announcement shocked markets. By mid-March, CBOT wheat prices lost 10% of their value. Money invested by funds on Wall Street into agricultural futures markets flowed out, and flowed into safe haven assets like US government bonds. As country after country went into lockdown, total grain demand declined. As an example of how this played out, people suddenly drove a lot less. The less they drove, the less fossil fuels they needed, and the less crop-based biofuels were needed to be blended in fuel tanks. To provide some context, biofuels in the present day are used largely as a way of reducing emissions in road transport, and increasingly in maritime and aviation industries too.

Markets seesaw

After the initial shock and wheat market sell-off, prices did a U-turn. Governments began stepping in to make large purchases of wheat to shore up their country's food reserves against potential supply chain disruptions. Governments wanted to make sure that no matter what, their population remained fed. This was especially the case for countries in North Africa and the Middle East who were large net importers of wheat. The Arab spring that was marked by anti-government protests, uprisings and rebellions was still fresh in the minds of policy makers. Concerns about food availability were compounded by the governments in some exporting countries blocking wheat exports to shore up their own supplies.

FROM COVID TO UKRAINE – A NEW GLOBAL CONFLICT IS BREWING

In the US, the operations of the grains industry remained largely unscathed in the early stages of the pandemic. In Europe, borders were closed to international arrivals on the 18th of March, but vessels importing food and animal feed continued to flow in. However, there were wide-scale and strictly controlled border checks in place between EU countries for the first time in decades. Border checks significantly slowed down the pace of European trade. What made matters worse was that workers were so afraid of being infected that they stopped showing up for work, creating considerable bottlenecks at key logistical hubs.

Russia, the world's largest wheat exporter, closed its international borders, and from March the 20th banned all grain exports for 10 days while the government took stock of the situation. The ban served two purposes. On the one hand, they were assessing how much grain was remaining in the country so that sufficient quantities were available for local use in the worst-case scenario. Second, the ban allowed local players like flour millers and food manufacturers to be able to stock up on reserves. The ban was prematurely overturned on the 24th of March.[44]

From a global perspective, while port disruptions were experienced at times, it has to be said that the global grains industry handled the initial months of Covid very well. Grain continued to flow to world markets largely undisrupted.

In Australia, the main challenge involved obtaining sufficient volumes of fertilisers and agrochemicals from overseas to get ready for the first large non-drought planting in years. Australia imports the vast majority of the inputs needed to grow crops, and a significant proportion of those come from China. Unfortunately for Australia, Hubei which was the epicentre of the Covid outbreak, was also the epicentre of Chinese herbicide, pesticide, and insecticide production. It reportedly accounted for one third of China's national production. The result was shipment delays of three to five weeks. The shipment delays were further compounded by a 14-day quarantine period on any vessels coming from China that was temporarily being enforced by the Australian government.

Unprecedented levels of government involvement in agriculture

Rarely in history did governments around the world get involved in agriculture more than they did at the beginning of Covid. From restricting exports, to buying local produce, to building up national reserves - the government suddenly sprung up everywhere.

The panic in international markets across the first half of the year also prompted governments to start looking at how they could permanently insert themselves into the grains industry. The Argentine government planned (unsuccessfully) to nationalise the nation's largest soybean exporter. Russia and Kazakhstan discussed whether they could create a wheat version of OPEC (Organisation of Petroleum Exporting Countries) to control grain prices and production. The idea of a wheat OPEC at the time may have seemed farfetched. However, it is important to note as per chapter two of this book that this concept was already tested by western countries in WWII via the International Wheat Agreement.

FROM COVID TO UKRAINE – A NEW GLOBAL CONFLICT IS BREWING

May heralded the beginning of a post-globalisation world for the Australian grain trade. Along with the US, Australia's relationship with China quickly deteriorated. It particularly worsened after Australia insisted on an investigation into the origins of Covid. At the time, China was the largest buyer of Australian barley by a long shot. On the 20th of May 2020, China implemented stiff anti-dumping tariffs on Australian barley exports. The tariffs made it economically unviable for Australian merchants to export to China. The tariffs were announced just as Australian farmers were in the process of finishing planting their next barley crops, making changes to planting decisions near impossible. In a very short time period Australian barley prices slid in value by a fifth. The anti-dumping tariffs caught many grain merchants, even the largest, off guard. Hundreds of millions of dollars were lost as cargos already on their way to China had to reroute and find cheaper destination markets elsewhere.

Beginning of the bull rush

Moving into the European mid-year harvest, the market was slow to realise there was a serious production problem brewing. Crop tours that usually shed light on production prospects were cancelled due to COVID. For context, crop tours are what they sound like, groups of people moving through cropping regions, usually in a minibus, assessing the potential harvest size. With no crop tours, it was a challenge to assess true production prospects – satellite imagery only helped to an extent. European production prospects were actually deteriorating, and fast. At this stage, the European wheat crop was forecast to come in at approximately 140 million tonnes. This was already a massive 12.5 million tonnes down on the previous harvest. Compounding declining production prospects in Europe, South America also became drier and production prospects began to shrink for corn and soy.

A sudden decline in the global production outlook coincided with the first easing of lockdowns in Europe and America. As people started to drive more, the total volume of biofuel that needed to be used in fuel tanks rose. Meanwhile over in China, fear of further global supply chain disruptions led to mass stockpiling. In an attempt to shore up everything from infant formula to grains - Chinese imports began to rise.

Australia truly does live-upside down

While global wheat prices were starting their journey up by mid-2020, Australian prices were doing the opposite and heading down. With the drought over and by September a large harvest only two months away, local prices plummeted from a peak of $500 AUD/tonne for milling wheat during the drought, to a low of $300/tonne by year end.

The price bull rages into October

During October, CBOT wheat prices rose by 11% to the highest level in almost a decade. Concerns over inflation due to large government stimulus and the search for higher returning assets by Wall Street led to a record wave of speculative and index fund investment into commodities.[42] From June onward speculative fund

FROM COVID TO UKRAINE – A NEW GLOBAL CONFLICT IS BREWING

investments in US wheat futures reached record net long positions. What's interesting is that while rising commodity prices would usually turn buyers off from buying more, in this scenario rising wheat prices were being met with ferocious buying through November.

2021 – Rapid price rise continues

Global wheat prices rose by a staggering 25% over the first month of 2021, and then another 20% by March.[42] The year started with drought developing over North America and the Black Sea countries. The Russian government was busy implementing an export tax on wheat to keep domestic wheat and food prices low by disincentivising exports. Global wheat stock estimates were down 4% by the end of January versus the prior year. In the EU, ending stocks were estimated at the lowest level in almost four decades.[50]

Meanwhile, the Chinese hog herd had recovered significantly. Associated with the hog herd recovery was rising feed grain demand and prices. Everything from corn to soy and wheat were pulled into Chinese feed rations. China's imports of corn quadrupled from 7.5 million tonnes the year prior to 30 million tonnes that year.

Such a surge in global prices meant that local Australian prices suddenly reversed their downward trajectory and started creeping back toward the high peaks that were set during the drought. It was unusual to have both a phenomenal production year and high wheat prices. In fact, the Australian wheat crop ended up being even bigger than expected, with just over 31 million tonnes being reaped at the end of 2020.[45] That harvest was almost the highest on record at that point.

WAR AND WHEAT

Vessel availability withers

For nations that needed to import their grain from overseas, things went from bad to worse. Not only were grain prices rocketing higher, but so were freight costs. The Baltic Dry Index, a global bellwether for the price of bulk freight hire, rocketed right past pre-pandemic levels. A combination of factors including a recovery in demand, COVID measures delaying vessel movements at ports, and unfavourable weather events around the world, led to the escalation of freight costs. This made the price of food for the end consumers living in importing nations even higher.

Prelude to the war in Ukraine

A brewing storm in March 2021 that most people weren't paying enough attention to, took the shape of Russia amassing 100,000 troops on its border with Ukraine. This was a year before the actual invasion. It was the largest movement of troops since Russia annexed Crimea in 2014. While many troops were eventually drawn back, much of the infrastructure for future deployment remained on the border with Ukraine.

Bullish price drivers keep piling up

The selling of wheat in Russia dried up in April as both farmers and grain traders tried to pressure the government to remove the export tax it implemented in 2020. At the same time, droughts were intensifying over North Africa, Europe, Brazil, and the US. American farmers were planting their spring wheat into dry soil. The accumulation of negative production news drove global wheat prices up another 15% over April. [42] The only bright spot was Australia, where most farmers were planting wheat into the best conditions seen for years.

Skipping forward a few months, in August, one month before harvest time in Canada, wheat crops were being sizzled under 40-degree temperatures. The shortage of grain eventually became so severe that Canada ended up importing malt barley (for brewing) from Australia. Just as Australia importing wheat during its drought was very uncommon, so was the case of Canada importing Australian barley.

By September, while the world was suffering from mass scale crop failures and rapidly depleting wheat stockpiles, Australia was moving into a wheat harvest that would break records, following an almost record-breaking result the year before. Australia wasn't far away from bumping into a very familiar theme – too much of a good thing.

Return of the Russian Army

In October, Russia began a second military build-up on the border with Ukraine. This time, however, there were more soldiers and infrastructure being deployed. Troops were being amassed not only in eastern Ukraine, but also in Belarus to the north of Ukraine and to the south in Crimea. The year ended with government officials in Russia and diplomats abroad repeatedly denying that Russia had any plans to invade Ukraine even though they continued to build up troops at the border.

WAR AND WHEAT

2022 – COVID morphs into the war in Ukraine

In early 2022 a large proportion of the developed world had been vaccinated and lockdowns were finally being lifted for good. The world appeared as though it was slowly moving back to normal. People were free to leave their homes and begin driving more. This increased the demand for grain and oilseeds used in biofuels (crop-based fuels). As economies recovered from the COVID shock, meat consumption also rose which increased the demand for grain to feed animals.

Meanwhile even though Russia had built up a large military presence on Ukraine's border by early February, many commentators were sceptical about whether an invasion was really inevitable. Many commentators just thought that it was a form of chest beating.

As we now know, those commentators were dead wrong. In the days leading up to Russia's official invasion of Ukraine on the 26th of February prices began to skyrocket. Once the invasion started, prices broke all-time records. By the 7th of March, CBOT wheat was up a staggering 88% compared to the 1st of January.[42] As a comparison, back in WWI it took several months for a similar rise in wheat prices to eventuate. The initial fear in the market was that there would be a complete and long-term cessation of all exports from the Black Sea. Russia and Ukraine accounted for roughly 20% and 10% respectively of global wheat exports at the time.

Exports out of all Ukrainian Black Sea ports were instantly stopped, and ports were mined off to avoid Russian invasion via the Black Sea. Ukraine could now only export small volumes of wheat over land to eastern

FROM COVID TO UKRAINE – A NEW GLOBAL CONFLICT IS BREWING

Europe. Russian ports were also initially shut off to trade, but they re-opened not long after being closed.

Stories were frequent of the Russian military taking expensive western farm machinery from eastern Ukraine and moving it back to Russia. Due to a voluntary withdrawal of machinery maintenance and parts delivery by western companies into Russia, Ukrainian machinery was being utilised for parts. Many stories arose from the initial cut off of western support to farm machinery in Russia, including a rumour that when western GPS was disconnected, an old soviet system of GPS was substituted in, but the machinery initially struggled to move in straight lines.

Following the concern over Ukraine's ability to export grain, attention quickly turned to Ukraine's ability to produce crops under war conditions. Conveniently, wheat had been planted during the prior October, which meant the vast majority of production could still be harvested. The question was primarily about whether grain would be harvested by Ukrainian farmers in unoccupied areas, or harvested in occupied territory and taken by the Russian government. As expected, farming was incredibly risky at the time. The boundary between Russia and Ukraine continued to shift on a day-by-day basis, making farming difficult to say the least. Photos started popping up on social media of farmers sitting in tractors with bullet proof vests on.

Fortunately for the year ahead, and for the spring crops that were yet to be planted, Ukrainian farmers already had more than half of their annual needs for fertiliser, agrochemicals, and seeds in storage. In the coming months, supply chains would continue to function when it came to crop inputs, but financial liquidity became a constant challenge for many Ukrainian farmers.

WAR AND WHEAT

A lot of desperately needed grain gets left in Ukraine

While attacks continued throughout Ukraine, ports were left largely untouched by Russian missile barrages in the beginning. Port facilities are of high value and take a long time to construct. The Russian government was likely to have been hoping to capture them upon their expected swift capture of Ukrainian port cities. Furthermore, the ports contained storage facilities with millions of dollars' worth of grain that could be sold on international markets.

On the 12th of March, western nations began rolling out a slew of sanctions, including on most Russian banks. While there were no sanctions placed on Russian food exports, including wheat, the sanctions on Russian banks caused considerable disruption. For example, the removal of Russia from the international interbank payment system called SWIFT made it far more difficult for Russian grain traders to transact and receive payments for their grain.

In theory, the west would have preferred to cut off as much Russian export activity as possible, including wheat, and starve it of foreign currency. However, cutting off the 20% of global wheat exports that Russia accounted for was not an option. With inflation starting to run hot globally, banning Russian wheat would have come at the worst possible time for western governments and central banks.

While initially Russian exports slowed due to a myriad of challenges ranging from lack of access to freight insurance, to cautious ship owners, and payment challenges, export flows quickly recommenced before too long. While many countries were initially reluctant to buy Russian wheat, there was a considerable number of countries including Tunisia and Egypt who simply couldn't afford to turn their back on Russian wheat. The main priority for those countries was feeding their population as cheaply as possible.

Western grain merchants continued to move Russian grain since it was not under sanctions. However, the vagueness and confusion at the time regarding what was and was not under sanctions led to many (particularly non-US) traders avoiding any dealings with Russian counterparts.

Boom goes the fertiliser

The global availability of crop fertiliser declined considerably with the onset of the war. Prior to the war, the concentration of global nitrogen fertiliser exports that came from Russia and Belarus equated to over a tenth of the total. The situation for potash fertiliser was worse, with an eye watering almost one third of global exports coming from Russia. For context, there are three key fertilisers needed for growing crops: nitrogen, potash, and phosphate.

The combination of an initial slowdown of fertiliser exports, panic buying of fertiliser across the globe and skyrocketing natural gas prices for Europe, led to skyrocketing fertiliser costs for farmers worldwide. As an explanatory note, natural gas is a major cost component in nitrogen production, and when Russia invaded Ukraine, flows of gas into Europe from Russia began to slow considerably. Prices of natural gas become so high that a significant proportion of European fertiliser factories had to temporarily shut down early in the war and stop producing nitrogen. The shortage in Europe started a domino effect through global supply chains.

WAR AND WHEAT

High wheat prices were here to stay

Wheat prices stayed at record levels throughout March as a reshuffle in global trade continued, and panic buying caused havoc worldwide. There were four consecutive days when trading was forced to halt on the Chicago Board of Trade due to the sheer magnitude of the price increases.

Net wheat importers, like Algeria, Tunisia, Iraq, Iran and Mexico saw large government wheat import tenders filled at very high prices without the usual haggling. This is what also happened leading into WWI and WWII.

The severity of the crisis meant that the times of continual growth in global grain demand were coming to an end. The USDA's estimates for global corn demand in the 2021/22 marketing year went from an expected growth of 5% on the year prior, to a 3% decline. That was the first decline that had been recorded in a decade.

The situation with prices being so high made it unsustainable for many businesses to continue operating without a significant rise in the price of their end product. The result was that consumer prices increased to compensate the food processors, and food price inflation began to take hold globally.

Russia's allies suffer

In Egypt, on average almost 60% of the annually consumed 20 million tonnes of wheat were imported, with more than 70% of that coming from Ukraine and Russia. Within one week following Russia's invasion of Ukraine, the price of unsubsidised Egyptian bread went up by more than 30%.

With Russia failing to seize Ukraine using the lightning style operation it thought would bring the country to its knees, and Ukraine suddenly receiving significant support from the west, both sides settled in for a long-drawn-out conflict.

Australia left behind as global prices rally

The wheat price rise in Australia since Russia's invasion of Ukraine was modest compared to the price gains made overseas. During the three-year drought between 2018 and early 2020, a large proportion of Australia's grain logistics infrastructure was idled due to insufficient grain volume. The problem was that the reduced logistical capacity that resulted coincided with a second consecutive massive crop that needed to be harvested at the end of 2021. That resulted in the problem of too much grain starting to rear its head as crop volumes overwhelmed supply chains. From rural areas where the grain was grown, to the ports where they were being shipped to overseas markets, grain was piling up everywhere.

Shipping slots were booked many months out. Grain merchants who wanted to ship more grain were physically constrained from doing so because there just wasn't the capacity within the infrastructure for it to happen. The oversupply meant that Australian wheat farmers had to wear a sizable price discount compared to global levels. And to the disbelief of many, the forecast was for a third consecutive year of plentiful rains for the coming cropping season.

WAR AND WHEAT

Australian Déjà vu

The similarities in the situation experienced in Australia following the first harvest during WWI, and in 2022 were uncanny. In both cases, a record amount of grain was harvested, and it substantially exceeded the capacity of the nation's logistical system for moving grain from rural areas to ports, and from ports onward to their final destination. Both harvests were abundant following horrific droughts where production suffered historic losses. During both periods, there were substantial challenges regarding the availability of shipping, and international freight costs were sky high.

2022 was the first year since 1914 when substantial volumes of Black Sea wheat supplies were lost due to a war. In both cases, the Black Sea accounted for roughly 30% of global wheat exports. In 1914, the wholesale price of Chicago wheat rose by over 70%, but it took several months following the start of WWI. Meanwhile, in 2022 CBOT wheat prices rose by 70%, but in this case it happened just a handful of days after Russia's invasion of Ukraine.

The main differences to note were the severity of the impact on the Australian grains industry. While production was at record levels in 2021, it was only marginally above the previous record reached in 2016, while in 1915/16 production was 70% above the last historic record.[4] Exports throughout 2022 were still able to continue, while following the 1914 harvest, shipping availability virtually disappeared due to the war. Ships were either sunk by Germans, requisitioned by overseas governments, or their owners feared coming Australia in order to not have their vessels requisition by the Australian government for military use.

FROM COVID TO UKRAINE – A NEW GLOBAL CONFLICT IS BREWING

In 1914, the total lack of availability of freight caused the government to nationalise the grains industry and create the Australian Wheat Board. The aim was to avoid the price farmers were receiving from collapsing and bankrupting them. More recently in 2021 and 2022, the private sector continued to operate, but the price received by growers was substantially lower than global levels. That said, it was still high from a historical context. The ability to ship grain remained, it was simply vastly insufficient compared to the harvest size.

Sanctions and market hesitancy made exporting a challenge for Russia

Russian exports of wheat were being impeded from two directions. First, vessels that would normally be heading in and out of Russia were finding it almost impossible to get insurance. The reason for that came down to insurance companies being unsure about how to price insurance arrangements for vessels moving through the Black Sea which was an active war zone. There was also the question of whether they should be insured at all. Furthermore, there was a general hesitancy for western insurance companies when it came to dealing with any trade that included Russia. This related both to the question of reputational damage, and from fear of accidentally contravening western sanctions.

Secondly, a large proportion of the agricultural and non-agricultural goods being shipped out of Russia had to be re-directed to the Black Sea due to a ban on the movement of Russian freight through EU countries. In turn, that resulted in a significant amount of congestion on the rail route to the Black Sea with the knock-on effect of increasing uncertainty around delivery times for buyers.

While prospects for the production of wheat in Russia and occupied eastern Ukraine were looking like a record, large questions remained over how much could actually export to world markets.

An inflation rollercoaster sets off for consumers

In March 2022, inflation in Australia hit its highest level in a decade. Meanwhile, the United Nations' Global Food Price Index reached its highest level since the 1990s.[47] Interestingly, food prices overseas rose more sharply than they did in Australia. It could be claimed, like in WWII, that part of the reason for lower food price inflation initially was due to Australia's insufficient logistics system. The bottleneck the Australian logistics system created for export, meant that more grain had to remain on the domestic market for longer, limiting the rise in local prices. A similar situation was experienced in WWII.

From this point onward, central bank interest rates started to rise rapidly across the world to rein in inflation, and in the process, reduce demand and the amount of speculative money flowing into agricultural markets.

A safe passage for Ukrainian grain

Meanwhile, discussions were taking place around the creation of a humanitarian grain corridor deal with Russia that would allow Ukrainian grain to safely move from their deep-sea ocean ports, through the Bosphorus

FROM COVID TO UKRAINE – A NEW GLOBAL CONFLICT IS BREWING

and into the Mediterranean. For now, Ukraine was only able to export a small proportion of their normal wheat volumes over land into eastern Europe. Not only were the volumes small, but they often created friction with local farmers who claimed Ukrainian inflows were lowering the price of their wheat. The continued deterioration of the South American corn crop and the US drought meant that an agreement about Ukrainian grain exports was critical to avoid a further rapid escalation of global food prices.

At the end of June, Russian troops agreed to depart Snake Island which is strategically positioned between Ukraine and the Bosphorus. The removal of this threat made way for a grain deal to be brokered between the two warring countries via the UN and Turkey. The deal allowed the Ukrainians to export goods safely out of its three main ports in the Black Sea without being attacked by the Russian navy. Russia on the other hand received concessions from the west. The concessions included the ability to receive payments for its grain exports via a US bank, and a promise that Russia would be helped with its aim of expanding the reach of its food and fertiliser exports.

Over the next year, global wheat prices fell as crops continued to flow out of Ukraine despite the occasional Russian missile targeting a Ukrainian port. There were other challenges too though. As part of the grain corridor deal, Russian inspectors would inspect all vessels at the entrances to the Bosporus strait heading into or out of Ukrainian ports. Russia wanted to make sure there was no military equipment coming into Ukraine disguised as a vessel picking up grain. When Russia felt that the west wasn't living up to its side of the

WAR AND WHEAT

deal, it would slow the inspections of Ukrainian vessels down to a crawl, causing a significant backlog. So even though vessels were leaving Ukraine, they weren't always getting far. Russia continued through the entirety of the deal to threaten it would pull out of the agreement.

By June 2023 global wheat prices slid to levels that were even lower than they were before the war. Remember that not only was Ukraine exporting, but at the time Russia was exporting record volumes of wheat following two consecutive record production years.

The humanitarian grain corridor deal eventually fell apart in July 2023 when Russia refused to re-sign the agreement. The Russian government continued to claim that the west failed to meet its demands. Markets initially reacted with a sharp rise in prices, but then returned to a gradual decline as exports continued to flow out of Ukraine over land to eastern Europe. Grain exports via the Danube River system in the south west of Ukraine also began to expand. By the end of 2023, Ukraine even organised the safe shipment of grain from its Black Sea ports by hugging the coast of neighbouring NATO countries. At the time of editing this book in mid-2024, Ukraine continues to export grain from its Black Sea ports despite continued attacks on ports and energy infrastructure.

CONCLUSION

CONCLUSION

'History Doesn't Repeat Itself, But it Often Rhymes'
Mark Twain

Once again we unfortunately find ourselves in an increasingly volatile world. War has broken out in Europe between Russia and Ukraine, and the potential for war in Asia continues to rise. Countries including China are actively working towards increasing self-sufficiency in food production. A trading block called BRICS, led by Russia and China, is attempting to move global trade away from the long-standing global reserve currency, the US dollar, and into their own currencies. Governments, including Australia's, are arguing that military spending needs to increase as a deterrence to potential adversaries. While none of those factors spell out 'broader conflict', they sure do sound familiar.

While there is little point speculating if a broader global conflict will occur (no one knows), it is important to ask whether the Australian grains industry would be any better prepared now than it was in the lead up to both world wars. This is the question I asked myself as I was getting close to the end of writing this book.

The answer to that question unfortunately, is no.

From the geographical perspective, Australia will always be dependent on ocean freight to ship our excess harvested crops to international markets. We simply don't have the kind of land borders that a country like Ukraine has to re-route exports via land in a situation where moving freight by sea becomes untenable. Furthermore, we have surprisingly few vessels to call upon in a national emergency. According to a Financial Times article published in 2022, the number of Australian owned commercial vessels can be counted on just two hands.[48]

From the perspective of how the grains industry has developed, domestic grain demand remains incredibly low compared to production. Over the last 10 years, Australia on average had to export 70% of its wheat production. That's equivalent to 19 million tonnes a year. In the case of Western Australia and South Australia, over 80% of their harvested crops were exported. On the east coast the proportion of total crops that has to be exported is smaller on average, but even so it still sits at about the 50% mark.

If there was ever to be a broader conflict again, freight availability would very likely evaporate again, and our local production would overwhelm local demand. The majority of crop produced would have no use domestically, or means of getting out of the country. Grains and oilseeds would simply pile up at storage sites and ports across the country. Unless the government became involved at that point, prices would sharply decline. The decline in prices would lead to mass bankruptcies in the farming sector, and gradually farmers would slowly leave the industry all together. While in the short term the decline in prices would be beneficial for local flour millers and the feed sector, it would very quickly result in grain production collapsing in the years that followed.

CONCLUSION

Unless there is fundamental change in the industry, it is hard to envision how the government would have any choice in a conflict other than resorting to the same strategies that it implemented in both world wars. In the event of a war, the government would need to implement a minimum price of wheat for farmers, sufficient to at least cover farmers cost of production. The government would take ownership of all grain. Grain merchants would need to become agents of the government, moving and storing grain under the decision making of the government. It would make no economic sense for grain merchants to own and simply hold grain in storage indefinitely on their own volition. Whenever freight would finally become available, the government would need to distribute it to the states proportionally, depending on how much surplus they have to export.

How do we avoid this scenario?

From where I sit, it's clear that to make the Australian grains industry more resilient to potential future conflict, there needs to be more domestic demand created for Australian crops.

The first, most obvious and historically proven avenue could be the development of a local biofuels sector. A biofuel sector would not only be an additional outlet for produced crops, but it would also allow the economy to function when fossil fuel oil isn't able to be imported in sufficient quantities. And as a reminder, Australia imports the vast majority of its fuel. In that context, it's important to note that local biofuel production would not make Australia entirely self-sufficient in fuel production, but at least our critical industries would be able to continue functioning if imports were to become unavailable. There is no doubt that the increasing electrification of road-based vehicles will make biofuels less relevant in the next 10-15 years when it comes to road transport. That said, it will remain very relevant for the aviation and maritime industries which cannot yet electrify. Furthermore, I assume here that there will be no conflict prior to the road transport fleet switching to electric cars.

While the biofuel industry can be developed by the private sector, government support will very likely be needed to give it a push. For those that may be opposed to using taxpayer funds to help create a biofuel industry, re-reading chapter one and two of this book should convince you why it is necessary. Building a biofuel industry during peace time may seem expensive, but building it during war time is far more expensive, if not impossible. During a war, construction costs would rise exponentially, while accessing skilled labour and equipment needed from overseas to construct the plants would become incredibly difficult. Without local biofuel production, we could be risking the entire economy grinding to a halt in the scenario where fossil fuel imports become unavailable.

While the development of a local biofuel industry would be beneficial in the scenario of a war, it would also be beneficial in times of peace for the farming industry. It would allow local crop prices to remain stronger and more insulated from overseas price volatility.

A second option to create a more resilient farming industry could be to export goods that require less freight. For example, an option worth considering is

CONCLUSION

expanding the grain fed animal protein sector. Roughly eight to twelve kilograms of grain creates one kilogram of beef. That means that in the scenario where less freight is available, exporting meat would be easier than grain from a tonnage perspective.

And so we come to a close. Instead of regurgitating my own thoughts again, I'll finish by re-using the below quote that was written in the year prior to WWII. I hope it inspires someone to take action.

"The curse of Australia is procrastination. We debate things in parliament eternally, but we hardly ever do anything." "I am afraid the awakening will be a rude one."
– J.M Harcourt January 1st 1938, Sydney morning Herald.

Questions and Answers with Dennis

1. What can readers do after reading your book?
   "Writing a review on LinkedIn, X/Twitter and amazon would be incredibly appreciated!"

2. If a reader wants to be on your update list, how can they sign up?
   "Send an email to vozagriculture@gmail.com with the subject 'Add me' in the title."

3. If a reader would like you to speak at their event about this book, how can they contact you?
   "They can email me at vozagriculture@gmail.com with the subject 'Event' in the title."

4. How can a journalist get in contact with you?
   "They can email me at vozagriculture@gmail.com with the subject 'Media' in the title."

5. If a reader wants to chat with you about the book, can they contact you?
   "Yes, just email me on vozagriculture@gmail.com or reach out on social media, I'm always happy to talk or grab a coffee!"

Acknowledgments

I would like to dedicate this book to my mum and dad. I also want to give a big thank you to my partner and broader family who had to suffer through years of endless history facts about grain.

Lastly, I would like to acknowledge the broader global network which I draw on frequently.

Notes

1. **Cox, W.** (2021) *London: A Global City in a Global Economy*, Demographia. Available at: http://www.demographia.com/dm-lon31.htm

2. **'Prohibition Against Aircraft'** (1914) *The Telegraph* (Brisbane, Qld.: 1872 - 1947), 4 August, p. 6. Available at: http://nla.gov.au/nla.news-article180483099

3. **'Britian's food supply'** (1914) *The Northern Star* (Lismore, NSW: 1876 - 1954), 4 August, p. 4. Available at: http://nla.gov.au/nla.news-article92047017

4. **Australian Bureau of Statistics** (2011) *7124.0 - Historical Selected Agriculture Commodities, by State (1861 to Present)*, 2010-11. Available at: https://www.abs.gov.au/AUSSTATS/abs@.nsf/DetailsPage/7124.02010-11

5. **Personal dataset based on aggregation of data from Australian rural newspapers**.

6. **'Enemy's food supplies'** (1914) *The Farmer and Settler* (Sydney, NSW: 1906 - 1955), 31 August, p. 1. Available at: http://nla.gov.au/nla.news-article111501539

7. **'Wheat seized** (1914) *The Australasian* (Melbourne, Vic.: 1864 - 1946), 18 September, p. 47. Available at: http://nla.gov.au/nla.news-article239609358

8. **'Food supplies** (1914) *The Australasian* (Melbourne, Vic.: 1864 - 1946), 18 September, p. 47. Available at: http://nla.gov.au/nla.news-article239609358

9. **'Trade and Finance'** (1942) *The Land* (Sydney, NSW: 1911 - 1954), 5 June, p. 3. Available at: http://nla.gov.au/nla.news-article154960038

10. **Federal Reserve Bank of St. Louis** (n.d.) *U.S. Wheat Area Harvested for Grain (M04F1AUS16980 M260NNBR)*. Available at: https://fred.stlouisfed.org/series/m04f1aus16980m260nnbr

11. **'Drought and the war** (1914) *The Age* (Melbourne, Vic.: 1854 - 1954), 27 November, p. 4. Available at: http://nla.gov.au/nla.news-article238887864

12. **'Trade and Finance** (1915) *The Argus* (Melbourne, Vic.: 1848 - 1957), 25 September, p. 6. Available at: http://nla.gov.au/nla.news-article155006005

13. **'Season's wheat – State Handling**(1915) *The Sydney Morning Herald* (NSW: 1842 - 1954), 10 November, p. 12. Available at: http://nla.gov.au/nla.news-article15623816

14. **'War prices** (1915) *The Sydney Morning Herald* (NSW: 1842 - 1954), 5 April, p. 5. Available at: http://nla.gov.au/nla.news-article15664362

NOTES

15. **'Keep the seas open'** (1915) *The Sydney Morning Herald* (NSW: 1842 - 1954), 8 December, p. 6. Available at: http://nla.gov.au/nla.news-article15629691

16. **'Shipping line'** (1916) *The Sydney Morning Herald* (NSW: 1842 - 1954), 29 June, p. 8. Available at: http://nla.gov.au/nla.news-article15647318

17. **'Cost of living** (1916) *The Sydney Morning Herald* (NSW: 1842 - 1954), 21 August, p. 13. Available at: http://nla.gov.au/nla.news-article15678128

18. **'Russians reduced acreage'** (1916) *The Sydney Morning Herald* (NSW: 1842 - 1954), 10 June, p. 10. Available at: http://nla.gov.au/nla.news-article15665512

19. **'Squeezing Belgium'** (1916) *The Sydney Morning Herald* (NSW: 1842 - 1954), 21 October, p. 9. Available at: http://nla.gov.au/nla.news-article15687978

20. **'Wheat problem** (1917) *The Sydney Morning Herald* (NSW: 1842 - 1954), 15 January, p. 8. Available at: http://nla.gov.au/nla.news-article15725976

21. **'World Food Shortage'** (1917) *The Sydney Morning Herald* (NSW: 1842 - 1954), 30 June, p. 9. Available at: http://nla.gov.au/nla.news-article15748018

22. **'Alcohol as a petrol substitute'** (1917) *The Sydney Morning Herald* (NSW: 1842 - 1954), 30 July, p. 8. Available at: http://nla.gov.au/nla.news-article15736678

23. **'Shipping and food** (1917) *The Sydney Morning Herald* (NSW: 1842 - 1954), 18 August, p. 6. Available at: http://nla.gov.au/nla.news-article15749428

24. **'Britian's food insurance'** (1938) *The Sydney Morning Herald* (NSW: 1842 - 1954), 11 February, p. 9. Available at: http://nla.gov.au/nla.news-article41615496

25. **'Wheat for storage'** (1938) *The West Australian* (Perth, WA: 1879 - 1954), 27 October, p. 4. Available at: http://nla.gov.au/nla.news-article46487073

26. **'Peace front in Balkans'** (1939) *The Sydney Morning Herald* (NSW: 1842 - 1954), 10 January, p. 6. Available at: http://nla.gov.au/nla.news-article17636353

27. **'Shipbuilding revival'** (1940) *The Sydney Morning Herald* (NSW: 1842 - 1954), 10 January, p. 5. Available at: http://nla.gov.au/nla.news-article17663000

28. **'Wheat glut in Canada'** (1939) *The Sydney Morning Herald* (NSW: 1842 - 1954), 28 December, p. 8. Available at: http://nla.gov.au/nla.news-article17635964

29. **'Widening of blockade'** (1940) *The Sydney Morning Herald* (NSW: 1842 - 1954), 29 July, p. 5. Available at: http://nla.gov.au/nla.news-article17680650

30. **'Activity in Africa'** (1940) *The Sydney Morning Herald* (NSW: 1842 - 1954), 5 October, p. 6. Available at: http://nla.gov.au/nla.news-article204385184

NOTES

31. **'Strategic Factors'** (1942) *The Courier-Mail* (Brisbane, Qld.: 1933 - 1954), 24 June, p. 2. Available at: http://nla.gov.au/nla.news-article47149626

32. **'Europe's Farthest Frontier'** (1941) *The Telegraph* (Brisbane, Qld.: 1872 - 1947), 11 October, p. 8. Available at: http://nla.gov.au/nla.news-article209812705

33. **'Limitation of wheat production'** (1940) *The Argus* (Melbourne, Vic.: 1848 - 1957), 3 July, p. 6. Available at: http://nla.gov.au/nla.news-article11984146

34. **'Control of farming'** (1942) *The Courier-Mail* (Brisbane, Qld.: 1933 - 1954), 7 January, p. 6. Available at: http://nla.gov.au/nla.news-article206847061

35. **'Reservoir of manpower'** (1941) *The Courier-Mail* (Brisbane, Qld.: 1933 - 1954), 16 September, p. 5. Available at: http://nla.gov.au/nla.news-article206349040

36. **'World Shortage of food'** (1941) *The Courier-Mail* (Brisbane, Qld.: 1933 - 1954), 1 October, p. 7. Available at: http://nla.gov.au/nla.news-article206353777

37. **'Rehabilitation of stricken nations'** (1941) *The Courier-Mail* (Brisbane, Qld.: 1933 - 1954), 11 November, p. 5. Available at: http://nla.gov.au/nla.news-article206344214

38. **'Hang on to what you've got, wheat growers'** (1944) *The Sunday Mail* (Brisbane, Qld.: 1926 - 1954), 19 September, p. 3. Available at: http://nla.gov.au/nla.news-article257995487

39. **'Invasion news'** (1944) *The West Australian* (Perth, WA: 1879 - 1954), 12 June, p. 6. Available at: http://nla.gov.au/nla.news-article44812463

40. **'Increased sowing'** (1945) *The Sunday Mail* (Brisbane, Qld.: 1926 - 1954), 8 September, p. 3. Available at: http://nla.gov.au/nla.news-article257991978

41. **'One-tenth Less, To Eat Than In 1939'** (1945) *The Sydney Morning Herald* (NSW: 1842 - 1954), 2 October, p. 1. Available at: https://trove.nla.gov.au/newspaper/article/17954749

42. **CME Group** (n.d.) *Wheat Futures*. Available at: https://www.cmegroup.com/markets/agriculture/grains/wheat.html

43. **United States Department of Agriculture** (n.d.) *PSD Online*. Available at: https://apps.fas.usda.gov/psdonline/app/index.html#/app/home

44. **Global Trade Alert** (n.d.) *Russian Federation: Temporary Export Ban on Grains Due to the COVID-19 Outbreak*. Available at: https://www.globaltradealert.org/intervention/79347/export-ban/russian-federation-temporary-export-ban-on-grains-due-to-the-covid-19-outbreak

NOTES

45. **Australian Bureau of Agricultural and Resource Economics and Sciences** (n.d.) *Australian Crop Report*. Available at: https://www.agriculture.gov.au/abares/research-topics/agricultural-outlook/australian-crop-report

46. **Reuters** (2019) *'China's Hog Herd May Drop by 55% from Fatal Swine Fever: Rabobank'*. Available at: https://www.reuters.com/article/us-china-swinefever-hogs/chinas-hog-herd-may-drop-by-55-from-fatal-swine-fever-rabobank-idUSKBN1WH2IG/

47. **Food and Agriculture Organization of the United Nations** (n.d.) *Food Price Index*. Available at: https://www.fao.org/worldfoodsituation/foodpricesindex/en/

48. **Fildes, N.** (2022) Australia warned it faces 'national emergency' as commercial shipping fleet dwindles. Financial Times, 21 March. Available at: https://www.ft.com/content/d1db32d1-91d1-4c5e-b427-b6a5ffa3d0df

Printed in Great Britain
by Amazon